Praise for
Stump the Librarian

"Alan Samry's *Stump the Librarian* is a deeply felt, extensively researched, and emotionally engaging work. The seemingly ordinary story of a librarian with a prosthetic leg becomes, in Samry's honest and eloquent telling, a remarkable journey through memoir, history, and literature. Journey along with this learned, soul-searching author."

—**Roy Hoffman**, Author of *Alabama Afternoons*, an essay collection, and *Come Landfall*, a novel

"Alan Samry's kaleidoscopic book, *Stump The Librarian* is at once a glorious compendium of quick biographies of one-legged individuals, a moving memoir, a fascinating history of amputations and prostheses, and a medical investigation of the congenital anomaly that left the author with a disability at birth. Samry, a librarian in Fairhope, Alabama, takes joy in the quest for answers and pursues information with the sublime sense of mission that the best librarians possess. With clarity, candor, and a down-to-earth directness, he takes us with him: fascinated, outraged, horrified, thrilled, and ever curious about a world populated—and profoundly changed—by those who not only get by on a single leg but stand far more firmly than many people with two. Samry weaves poignant personal recollection through his tapestry of information, making Stump The Librarian a must read."

—**Molly Peacock**, author of *The Analyst* and *The Paper Garden*

"I laughed and cried over the unique experiences of amputees. Hilarious and heartbreaking! I have been a Certified Prosthetist for nearly 20 years. I thought I knew a lot about amputees both personally and historically, but this book proved that there is more learn. This book is a fabulous collection of stories that captures the culture's perception and fascination of amputees. From mythical accounts to obscure historical records, Samry paints a picture in his book that brings these people to life! He has found a unique way to weave his personal story as having congenital limb deficiency with the other stories of amputees he has researched and met along the way. He gives a raw and transparent glimpse into life as an amputee. This is a must read for people who are touched with limb loss. I would recommend parents reading this book first prior to letting their young children read it due to some age sensitive content. This book is easy to read, and the format of the book makes it easy to put down and pick up as time allows."

—**Lisa J. Miller,** Certified Prosthetist, Certified Fitter-mastectomy, Eastern Shore Orthotics and Prosthetics, President of Alabama Prosthetics and Orthotics Association.

"Alan Samry takes readers on his personal journey of curiosity, humor and exploration. In an unlikely narrative, readers learn about Alan's life as a congenital below-knee amputee. In a very delightful and provocative manner, Alan relates his personal memoirs and shares historical and imagined characters who are like-amputees.
Alan's writing style is fascinatingly varied, and insightful into his own self-discovery. He shares intimate details that enable readers to appreciate his story and perspective.
This book is a celebration of Alan – his person, determination, and his insatiable desire for truth."

—**Tamara Dean**, Director, Fairhope Public Library

Stump the Librarian:
A Writer's Book of Legs

Alan L. Samry

ALAN L. SAMRY

Stump the Librarian Copyright © 2019 by Alan Samry
All rights reserved

"Three Legs of a Bedroom Life" appeared in *Disability Studies Quarterly*. "The Last Peg Leg" appeared in the *Birmingham Arts Journal*. "Shedding Our Shells" was published by *Obsession: An Online Literary Magazine*. "One Nation, Divisible" was published online by *The Dead Mule School of Southern Literature*. "$64.95" appeared in the *Falmouth Enterprise*. "The Gulf War" appeared in different forms in the *Falmouth Enterprise* and the *Fairhope Courier*. "To SMS" appeared in the *Falmouth Enterprise*. "Walking Aids" and "At the Corner of Fourth and York Outside the Louisville Free Public Library," were published in *Kaleidoscope* magazine. "Beauty Scars" was published in *Oracle Fine Arts Review*. Other stories and essays were published online at StumpTheLibrarian.com.

ISBN 9781945190346
FV-5HB

Cover Photography by Judy Bishop-Woods
Cover artwork by Michael Illaqua
Back Cover Photograph by Susan Samry
Cover logo by Megan Redlich
www.IntellectPublishing.com

Dedication

For my wife, Susan:
My muse, my teacher, and best reader
For librarians: especially my co-workers
For amputees: past, present, and future

ALAN L. SAMRY

Author's Note

This book is a cross-genre collection of creative writing. The chapters are organized as though the readers were in a public library. A piece of creative writing, children's book, a poem, a lyrical essay, or short story begins each chapter. It is mostly a work of creative nonfiction. Using memoir, biography, essay, analysis, and experimental writing it tells my story and the real and sometimes mythical stories of other amputees, living and deceased. The events are portrayed to the best of my memory.

While the stories in this book are true, it may not be entirely factual. Some names have been changed to protect privacy. Dialog has been recreated and chronologies have been condensed or compressed for narrative pacing and literary effect.

There are uncredited quotes at the beginning of each chapter and interspersed throughout the book to try and stump the reader. Some are familiar, but many more are obscure, so an answer key is located at the back of the book.

Although I would love for you to read it straight through, I invite readers to "hop around," and explore my library of legs.

AUG 23 2018

[signature]

ALAN L. SAMRY

Table of Contents

ALAN L. SAMRY

Stump the Librarian:
A Writer's Book of Legs

ALAN L. SAMRY

Prologue—A Library Branch Without Limbs

A. "Human nature is tribal; we seek other humans as we attempt to reconnect to fading memories."

I drop my backpack at the reference desk at the Fairhope Public Library. I fire up the two computers at reference and the three catalog computers around the desk. The desk is located behind sixteen computer stations in pods of four in the middle of the Colony Reading Room amidst the reference books.

"What's my PIN?" the man with black ink tattoos of two different women's names running down the hairless undersides of his forearms asks politely. He's trying to log into a computer with his library card.

"Last four digits of the card," I say, while looking through old newspapers for a patron about the fire at the library. After being open for just 44 days, the 39,600-square foot, two-story brick library on the corner of Fairhope Avenue and Bancroft Street was struck by lightning Tuesday, February 13, 2007. I was hired four months later and was going to school to earn my undergraduate degree at the University of South Alabama.

An older man asks, "Where can I find a copy of *America the Beautiful*?"

"Katharine Lee Bates wrote it," I say, "She lived in Falmouth, Massachusetts, where I grew up. Her house was just off the town green." Small talk while I look it up in the catalog. No immediate hits.

I learn that "alabaster cities" refers to the 1893 World's Fair in Chicago, which is also known as the White City, as it was modeled on Ancient Greek architecture. This little factoid was missing from one of my favorite books, *The Devil in the White City* by Erik Larson. Larson's book tells the parallel tales of hope and despair as he tracks the construction and events of the World's Fair with those of America's first serial killer. My coworker Pam and I are always amazed at how much history connects to the Chicago World's Fair. I wear an artificial leg every day, so my favorite part of the book was reading that many American artificial limb manufacturers displayed their wares in booths at the fair, including AA Marks and Bly.

All 16 computers are in use. Time: 10:06 AM.

Jay Qualey, a retired English Literature professor, stops by daily to tell me what he's reading. A white-haired guy in his 70s who looks like Mr. Snow, the brother of Mr. Heat Miser, Jay is usually reading at least three books at a time. Jay gives me a *Frank and Ernest* comic. Three pirates talk on board a ship. One pirate says to another about the third, who stands on a peg leg and has a contraption on his left arm, "He's the most obsessively neat captain I've ever worked for — he has a Dust Buster instead of a hook." I did a book review for *Treasure Island* a few years ago, and Jay knows about my obsession with anything one-legged.

In fact, lots of the staff know about my desire to read anything one-legged. Jane, my coworker in circulation, emailed a story about *Molly the Pony*, a Louisiana pony who lost her leg after a dog bite and was fitted with a prosthesis.

"We already have the book," I told her. I email Jane the picture of Molly, me, and Susan at Page and Palette, our local bookstore.

It's getting close to lunchtime and Cheryl, the reference manager and my supervisor, comes by the desk to tell a story about her Kentucky family. I'm not altogether sure how crazy they are-the ones I've met seem real nice-but Cheryl, who coined the phrase "yak-a-bell," always has a great story to tell.

"Jay, 'irregardless' is a word," Cheryl says.

"Not in my dictionary," he sasses back.

In the article, "In Defense of Irregardless," Tim Moynihan jokes how Merriam Webster says "it should not be used." Moynihan asks, "Can you name another word that the dictionary says you shouldn't use?"

In our print version of the *Oxford English Dictionary* (OED), which I walk by dozens of times every day, the word "stump" has the opposite problem. It's so overused it has five pages of entries. The first definition, "The part remaining of an amputated or broken-off limb or portion of the body" dates back to 1375.

The OED has 17 entries for the verb "to stump." The first use occurred in 1834, in a letter from C.A. Davis, "My Good Old Friend, – I'm stumped."

"To cause to be at a loss; to confront with an insuperable difficulty; to nonplus," according to the OED, which adds that, "the primary reference was probably to the obstruction caused by stumps in ploughing imperfectly cleared land."

It is rather easy to stump this librarian. I had to look up insuperable. It means "unconquerable, invincible." Oddly, there is no mention or use in the OED for the phrase "stump the librarian," though it's been bantered about by librarians and patrons for decades.

In my second semester of online library school at the University of Alabama it happened. I was reading page 115 of *Reference and Information Services: An Introduction*, by Cassel and Hiremath.

> "In the past, the stouthearted librarians of the New York Public Library would prove this time and time again as they ventured into schools to play the game, 'Stump the Librarian.'"

Clack of keys, clunk of a space bar on computer number 6. Cell phone ring tone. The library is no longer a quiet place to curl up with a book. It is the lifeblood of the community, buzzing with activity for many people. On average, we have 78 people per hour enter the library. The reference department handles hundreds of questions each week, ranging from book recommendations to catalog searches, and technology. At least once a day I help upload a photo onto an online dating site, into an email, onto ebay, Facebook, or Craigslist. At least once an hour someone shoves a smart phone in front of me asking me how to do something like print, move photos, or get eBooks. It's all good; knowing and staying current with technology is job security.

Our library director, Tamara Dean, is related to John Bell Hood, a major Confederate general in the Civil War who was amputeed in 1863 at the Battle of Chickamauga.

As I'm finishing up with a patron, a man rolls up in a wheelchair. I notice he's missing part of his left leg.

"Can I help you?"

"I'm looking for books about the Constitution," the white bearded and T-shirted man in his 60s grizzles.

"Okay, we've got a few things I can show you. Do you want to follow me down to the section in nonfiction or would you like me to bring some books up here for you?"

"I'll wheel down there with you," he says, sounding less irritated for having been given a choice.

I walk beside his wheelchair and take the lead as we enter the nonfiction section. Vincent Price! That's who he reminds me of as I show him an assortment of books at 372.73 and 973.4.

When he rolls by the desk on his way to check out, I notice he has *The Constitution of the United States of America* by Beverly Harcourt in his lap.

"Look, you and I have something in common," I say, raising my right leg off the floor and lifting my right pant leg.

I look at his stump, which is wrapped in a brown shrink sock and ends below mid-thigh.

"Nice," he says. "Above knee?" he asks me, looking at the black carbon fiber post and foot.

"No, below," I say, adding, "It was a birth defect." He gave me a nod, like he'd heard that story before.

"This is from a spider bite," he says, so matter of fact that he stares at me and watches my eyes light up. What kind of spider was it? My mind flashes as I think about the brown recluse, the most lethal arachnid around here. I don't ask. We are in the middle of the library. I think of the sign I saw over a bathtub that reads, "Knowledge speaks, Wisdom listens." With the stained-glass owl watching over me, I listen.

"It turned gangrene," he pauses, "they amputated it in February."

"Have you been fitted?" Knowing that older people have difficulty adjusting to amputations and some never get comfortable wearing a prosthesis.

"Yeah," he says, "I try to put it on once a day." I get the feeling in his softened voice that he is going through the motions but is mentally beaten.

"You in much pain?"

"I'm going to a pain doctor this week too." I've read a little about phantom pain, but this guy lost his leg to a spider bite. The scenarios the human mind can make up to adjust for loss is frightening. His leg is gone, but his mind and his nerves act like his leg is still there.

"I've been reading about mirror therapy for phantom pain," I say, "you might want to ask your doctor about it."

"Oh, I will and thanks for everything," he says.

"You've come a long way in just four months, so keep it up," I tell him, and force a smile as I think about what we don't have in common as we part ways.

As he rolls away it occurs to me that I'm passing. Oh sure, I walk with a limp, but most people don't know I'm an amputee.

Working part time at a public library is providing me with the opportunity to earn a real leg-ucation. My undergraduate degree provided a historical leg up, while my MFA in creative writing helps me tell my legs of life, and my Master's in Library Studies at the University of Alabama is the capstone that connects the stumps, the libraries, and the community. I like to read about missing legs, tell and hear stories about legs, but most of all I like to write about legs.

A few years ago, Cheryl told me the story of her father, Mr. Smith, chain sawing off his own leg. Maybe one day I'll meet her dad and hear his version of what happened. Until then, here are some stories from my life, and amputees, biographical, mythical, and fictional, whose legs I found in the library.

Me, with Kaye Harris, Molly's caretaker, and my wife, Susan (far right) outside Page and Palette Bookstore.

ALAN L. SAMRY

1.Youth Services

B. "When I was growing up no one was giving me magazines for people with disabilities. It wasn't a tribe or an identity…What I do know is the common, universally shared experience of knowing what it's like to feel different."

Me, my brother Steve, and the go-go dancers

The Uniped and the Mermaid

Pedro was not like all the other pirates on the ship called *Bones*. He was a uniped and had only one leg and one foot.

One day he saw a mermaid, wiggling in the waves.

Pedro did not believe what Captain Redbeard said about mermaids. He said they cursed pirates, took their gold, and drowned them at the bottom of the sea.

"Help me!" the mermaid cried from beneath the rolling sea, but the captain sailed on. Pedro didn't want to be a pirate. He wanted to be free and to help the mermaid.

He hopped off the ship, and pierced the water's surface, without a splash, not even a ripple.

Pedro was fast in the water, a one-legged aqua boy swimming quickly, cutting the surface as quickly as a water spider flicking its legs. He stuck his head beneath the sea.

"My name is Muria. Neptune, the merman, has me clamped to this old anchor chain," she said. The lock was shackled around her tail where her fin began to fan. Muria asked, "Can you swim far underwater and free me from the pain of these chains? Like the whale, I need to breathe air too, and soon!"

"Yes," Pedro croaked. He was nervous and had a frog in his throat.

"Follow me to the bottom of the sea," Muria said. She found his hand and held it tight as they dived down. Suddenly, he was no longer holding his breath. He was breathing underwater! Pedro felt goosebumps. Muria said, "You are alright."

Pedro looked down and saw the sandy bottom of the ocean floor, and he swam circles round Neptune and bent each tine of his trident. He unlocked the shackle by turning the key. He set Muria free.

They swam as fast as dolphins, on and on. Then they dined on krill and phytoplankton.

Muria and Pedro swam away together, holding hands, facing each other, as friends who look out for one another.

A Peg to Stand On

"You were trying to stand on one leg," Mom remembered. She said I would plant the end of the stump into the crib mattress for balance. Then I would grab onto the wooden slats and lift myself up.

"You'd topple over," she said, grinning at the image of me in her memory, "but then you'd try it again."

"If Shriners didn't give you a leg to stand on to begin walking with, you were going to crawl to China," Mom recalled.

My first visit to Shriners Hospital for Crippled Children, in Springfield, Massachusetts, was in July 1968. After a private evaluation, I was "seen" by doctors and nurses during a Limb Deficiency Clinic. Dr. Toutounghi ordered up the specifications for my first prosthesis. "Alan is to be fitted with a plastic laminate or wooden socket depending on which is easier for Mr. Williams to do with an above the knee strap and waist band. He will not have a foot on the prosthesis."

The first time Dr. Kruger saw me at Limb Deficiency Clinic, in October 1968, he was appalled. Dr. Kruger's frustration was spoken into a Dictaphone, and then typed into my record:

"There is no stability of the socket on the stump and cosmetically the result is miserable. I don't understand why such a prescription was permitted to go out of this clinic, there has never been such a prescription before and I am disturbed by it."

I picture Dr. Kruger yelling this in his deep, gravelly voice.

"It was plunger-like," Mom said, when I asked her about the first peg. When we talked about how I got around on it, she said I really didn't, at first.

"You had trouble figuring out how to stand up when you had the peg on. I think it was because by then you had already

14

figured out how to stand up without the peg. At first, we would pick you up and let you stand on it. Then you went back to the old way of pulling yourself up on that good leg. You were puzzled by the prosthesis," she said.

A day after my first birthday, November 22, I was given a present at Shriners. It was my first foot, a SACH (Solid Ankle Cushion Heel).

"You planted that foot, held onto the sofa and moved your good foot." When she told me, I thought of the funky James Brown song, "Get on the Good Foot."

"All your brothers and sisters would take turns holding your hands, helping you take those first steps. With arms open across the room, they'd say 'Come on, Alan.' You'd walk to them. That leg was a little short because you were growing so fast. I remember you planted your weight on that first foot you had. You trusted it."

In May 1969, I was 16 months old, weighed 32 pounds, and measured 32 inches long. Waiting to be seen by the doctors and nurses at the clinic, Mom sat with me in the "next up" seating area, which was located in the hallway next to the hospital check-in desk.

"He is walking all over the place and it holds on beautifully," Dr. Fisher reported.

"You still crawled when you didn't have your prosthesis on," Mom said, "but you were already trying to balance yourself, standing on one leg."

Three months later Dr. Paul said, "This boy is running all over the place in his prosthesis." Sometime after my third birthday and before my fourth, Mom said I wasn't crawling much anymore.

"You were hopping everywhere."

My Only Wholly-Limbed Nauset Memory

Exactly 347 years before my birthday, the Pilgrims arrived on Cape Cod, "A hideous and desolate wilderness full of wild beasts and wild men," according to William Bradford. While explorers, pioneers, and later Americans were obsessed with heading west, a faction of the Plymouth Colony Pilgrims ventured east toward the rising sun. They sent a committee, including future governor Thomas Prence, to explore the area where Pilgrims first encountered Wampanoag Indians on Cape Cod in 1620. The Pilgrims maintained relations and traded for food with Nauset leader Aspinet. Although most think of Cape Cod today as a strip of sand, Bradford noted in *Of Plimouth Plantation*, that the Nauset soil, "is for the most part blakish [sic] and deep mould, much like that where groweth [sic] the best tobacco in Virginia." He was referring to the area around Fort Hill in the town of Eastham, which was incorporated as Nauset in 1646. Some of the early Nauset settlers were kids on the *Mayflower*.

I was in attendance at the 350th anniversary of First Encounter Beach, site of the first contact between Pilgrims and Wampanoag. I was only three so I don't actually remember, but I have the photo to prove it. We are on the beach and lots of kids from Eastham Elementary School are wearing paper headbands with seagull feathers sticking up from the back. I'm sitting on my brother Mark's legs, his hands are crossed over my lap. My brother's friend and our neighbor, Hank Curtis, is smiling at me, touching my chin. The camera captures my grin. Looking at the picture, I can't see beyond my vertically-striped pants and the jacket with a hood that was zipped up over the top of my head. No one at the beach that day would guess that I had an artificial leg on.

First Encounter Beach, Eastham. In my brother Mark's lap with Hank Curtis

We couldn't see or hear the Atlantic Ocean from the historic house my family rented in Eastham in the early 1970s. I remember the smell and taste of salt, which lingered like dew in heavy air. The Atlantic, my dad was fond of saying, was less than a mile "the way the crow flies" over Nauset Harbor. My mom still refers to the first house I remember as the "Graves' house," named after the owners who lived on Governor Prence Road just a few hundred yards down Route 6. The rectangular living room extended from the front to the back of the house. It was painted a strange shade of blue. Not baby. Not navy. The front or west side of the room was the high traffic area because it led to the stairs, my parents' bedroom, and the front door we never used. The rubber literally hit the road about twenty steps from our front door. Four lanes of speedy Route 6 traffic sped by within a few yards of the house. There was a small drop a few feet from the fieldstone front step and a few overgrown bushes near the road. On the north side of the property was a big sign: Fort Hill Next Right. A mile or so west was First Encounter Beach.

A couple years later, I began exploring the same areas as the Nauset founders. Of those years living in Eastham, I treasure one particular adventure with my sister Lynne. The day is not special because of landscape, spending time with family, or exploring new territory, though those details are still vivid and precious. In Algonquian, Nauset means "at the place between," and that's where I found myself.

***

With Dad, at the Graves' House, Route 6, Eastham

I watched my mom one day from my bedroom, a small room off the living room, which was called the borning room in old Cape Cod houses. Mom's wavy, brown, shoulder-length hair was bobby-pinned to a red paisley bandana covering the top of her head like a kerchief. The blue housecoat she always wore brought out the color of her eyes, which turned hazel like a mood ring when she was angry or upset.

When I walked into the living room, I heard the creaking of the ironing board and saw her work uniform on the back of the sofa. She quickly wielded the all-metal, black handled iron over the black apron, white blouse, and black knee-length skirt for her waitressing job at Laurino's Restaurant, a very busy pizza place on Route 6A in Brewster. A lit Pall Mall or Tareyton hung from her lips and a late, liquid breakfast, probably a screwdriver, rested on the wide end of the ironing board alongside the iron's fraying cloth-covered cord.

"Take Alan outside with you," Mom told my nine-year-old sister, Lynne, just after she hit the bottom of the stairs with a two-footed thud. Lynne had thick, straight, dark-brown hair, a small button nose, thin lips, and blue eyes. She was in a pair of patchwork pants and a windbreaker. Lynne was a Campfire Girl and lived their Indian-sounding motto, WoHeLo, short for work, health, and love.

"Okay, Ma," was all Lynne said. I followed her toward the kitchen, dressed in blue and white vertical-striped pants, a plaid flannel shirt and a pair of brown Hush Puppies. We walked through the kitchen, past the bathroom with the toilet that never worked, and out the back door.

We had a huge back and side yard. The leaves on the frowning branches of the tall weeping willow trees rattled like deadly snakes in the ever-present wind. The forsythia had changed from its seasonal golden flush to the green of summer. The driveway was a dirt and sand pathway rutted by tires. The middle was a humped jumble of grass and weeds. We each took a tire rut as we set out to explore.

On the Atlantic side were the blackberry vines growing wild between our house and Mrs. Chase's, whom we visited often, for which we were rewarded with freshly baked cookies. The wild berries grew in a tangled thicket of poison ivy and briars that bore only thorns. Lynne had long fingers and was a better picker, but more importantly, she had an eye for what was ripe. There is nothing worse than expecting a mouthwatering gush of sweetness, only to get a bitter bust. Seeing the look on my face, she'd hand me another and pick some extras to eat along the way.

South of the house was Cove Cemetery, where we played over the bones of Pilgrims. There were two large trees in the middle of the cemetery: an evergreen, and another that still didn't have any leaves. We used to walk into the cemetery through the opening of a concrete and steel fence near the front. We jousted with fallen sticks that snapped at every strike. The grave markers served as hiding places where we would crouch down behind the carved stones to hide from each other. Even as a kid, I knew that people who came on the *Mayflower* were buried in the cemetery. Lynne read the markers of Constance Snow, Joseph Rogers, and Giles Hopkins. The Reverend Samuel Treat had a monument, but Lynne said he was not a *Mayflower* passenger.

Lynne and I were headed north: Fort Hill. The tree line to the north of the house was dark. We entered the forest with the din of humming traffic in the distance. We walked the worn black-soiled path. Ferns as tall as me were growing everywhere. The trees, some large, some just skinny saplings struggling for sun in the cool shade canopy, included oaks, pines, and maples.

"Are Joe, Dede, and Tata here, Alan?" Lynne wanted to know who else was joining us. While she giggled, we stopped to look at a pink lady slipper, its bulb dangling just above the dirt.

"No, I don't know where they are," I said. Lynne was always uneasy until I responded. It was hard to compete with your little brother's imaginary friends. Lynne was the only person who talked to them. The path came out alongside the Curtises' garage. Hank Curtis had an old green motorbike, minus the motor, with short fat wheels that we used to ride down hills.

We walked on the pavement where Route 6 forked with Governor Prence Road. The shoosh, woosh, vroom, and vibration of every vehicle made us quicken our pace. My steps felt strange on the pavement. Lynne leaned into me and drove me onto the shoulder where blades of green and brown grass popped up through the sand like chin stubble. Just past Mary Chase Road, on both sides of the road, there were tall grasses, milkweeds, and cattails with brown fuzzy tops. A few minnows darted away as we looked into the small creek under Governor Prence Road.

Except for the wind rustling the leaves over our heads, it was suddenly very quiet. A comfortable silence between siblings came over us; perhaps we wondered what awaited us upon our return. The road curled back towards Route 6 and on the right, past a low fence with circle shapes between the top and bottom rails, stood a huge home. The Captain Edward Penniman House was not just a historical landmark inside the National Seashore boundaries, it was our discovery. The midday sun cast a shadow over the front of the house and trees shaded the back and the side yard. The front and side yards were terraced with stone walls so the land around the house was raised above the roadways. It looked massive and was like no other house I'd ever seen. It was tall, square, and painted yellow. The gray or black weather-beaten wood shingles of most Cape homes were absent. The short steep hill outside the fence seemed a nice place for a detour. We played tag in the grass just outside the fence. I lay down in the grass and rolled down the hill. If that didn't disorient us enough, we spun around when we stood up. Rolling was fun in the clover, dandelions, and leaves. Penniman House, grass, sky, trees, Penniman House. We got silly and rolled over each other until someone got hurt. We'd stop for a minute and roll again.

"You're gonna get sick," Lynne said, as I staggered to my feet looking as green as the grass.

We followed the road and fence line to the left—up Fort Hill Road with the house to our right. The wooden fence ended, and a whitewashed rock wall ran along the side of the property. As we crested the small hill, the rock wall ended at two curved white poles.

"What is that thing?" I must've thought to myself. It was four of me tall. I looked up into the midday sun at this mysterious thing. I smelled paint. The arch or gateway was held up by two wooden posts. I didn't walk under it. Judging by the worn area in the grass outside this thing, it seemed like a lot of people chose not to go through the gateway. Maybe it was bad luck, like walking under a ladder.

"It's a whale jawbone," Lynne said. She was older, knew everything, and had probably been there before or heard it from a friend. I'd never seen a whale. If this was just a jaw, how big is a whole whale? What kind of whale was it? She didn't know. The whalebone had a grain like wood with holes in it with slivers missing. I felt the ridges on the massive jaw bones, shaped like crescent moons almost connecting together at the top. A metal bolt that was supposed to connect the two pieces at the top was broken, leaving a gap that somehow seemed natural. The surface had tiny little holes in it; I wondered if you poured water on it, if the bone would drink it up. I was curious about this whalebone. I planned to come back, again and again, to look at it and study it. Most of all, I wondered why the whaling captain put it there.

In the back yard of the Graves' House in Eastham. Mark, Lynne, me, Laurie (First Communion), and Steve

Who Is Benito Badoglio?

"Did you ever read this?" my wife, Susan, asks me. We are at Reed Books, in Birmingham. The Museum of Fond Memories in downtown Birmingham, Alabama, is a destination no bibliophile, antiquer, or ephemera collector should miss. It's best not to look. Let an item find you as you wind, meander, and wend your way through a sarcophagus of paper entrails.

I glanced at the cover; it didn't look familiar.

"No, I don't think so."

As it was one of Sue's favorite books as a child, her eyes lit up recalling the adventures of the main character and how much she knew I was going to love the book. She handed it to me to look at, but I refused, saying, "Just buy it."

The Hat, written and illustrated by Tomi Ungerer, was published in 1970 and quickly fell out of print, but it continues to be a highly rated and sought-after children's picture book.

It wasn't until Saturday night, back home in Fairhope, that we finally got around to reading the book.

"Read *The Hat* to me," I said to Sue as we sat together on the love seat in our living room.

The book cover doesn't show you much, it's just a bunch of colorful heads looking up at a hat; but when you turn to the cover page there is man in a weathered soldier's uniform with chin whiskers, crutches, wearing a peg leg and a charming hat. Okay, so I'm totally intrigued as Sue starts reading.

"A tall black top hat, shiny as satin
and belted with a magenta silk sash."

The hat comes alive on the head of our main character, Benito Badoglio, a down-on-his-luck veteran. The hat begins doing good deeds and saving people from physical harm, and Benito is the beneficiary of their generosity.

24

"With his rewards Benito Badoglio bought clothing to match his hat."

Sue turned the page. Benito was transformed!

"He had his peg leg fitted with a silver wheel."

Badoglio's kicking up dust in his practically preposterous wheeled prosthesis. The crutches are gone, replaced by a highfalutin, yet functional cane. I wish I knew of this book when I was a child because I was fascinated with wheels. Matchboxes, Hot Wheels, Big Wheels, training wheels, bicycles, and especially skateboards. We did not have many books in our home. We went to the library occasionally, but we were not a family of book readers. When I played with cars, lying leg-free in the dirt beside the driveway, I was in a world of my own. I can only wonder where Benito Badoglio's silver wheel would have taken me.

An Amputee's Leg and Steam Shovel's Arm

C. "So I figure if the entire world is one big machine, I have to be here for some reason. And that means that you have to be here for some reason, too."

Mike Mulligan and His Steam Shovel, written and illustrated by Virginia Lee Burton, used to fill me with wonder and fuel my imagination. I thought I was over the book, you know, been there, done that, bought the T-shirt. I was wrong. Even now, the story brings back memories, conjures the imagination, and sparks my creativity.

One of the best parts of the book is the diagram of the steam shovel with her name, "Mary Anne," emblazoned on the "boom." The "dipper," or bucket, is labeled from top to bottom as "teeth," "dipper," and "tongue." Mike and Mary Anne are the best digging duo the city has ever seen. They scoop earth and "finish the corner neat and square."

Mary Anne wears her personification on her dipper, with subtle human eyes, smiling mouth, big eyelashes, and even tears. Mary Anne's dipper has fabulous facial expressions that match the action on the page, from grimaces and grins, to batting eyelashes, closed mouthfuls of dirt, and mouth agape as dirt drops in brown clouds to the ground.

Burton's sweeping brush stroke illustrations, in a seven-year old's imagination, move on the page as the shifting boom billows white steam and the black puffs from the "smokestack" blot the sky.

My prosthetic leg has characteristics similar to Mary Anne's shovel. The leg is a lever, or simple machine, and built of manmade materials: metal, plastic, fiberglass, and wood. My motion with a prosthesis, while not machine-like, is certainly awkward, and my gait looks a lot like Mary Anne's swinging arm.

Eventually, technology catches Mary Anne, and she and Mike are overtaken by more efficient gas and diesel shovels. So Mary Anne and Mike's journey takes them from urban to rural areas, while my trip with Mom to Shriners Hospital took me in the opposite direction. Types of communities, according to my wife, Susan, are still something second graders learn. (I'm writing this in her classroom, which has a copy of *Mike Mulligan and More*. She teaches at Daphne East Elementary, but this is summer, and she's in a lesson-planning meeting with her fellow second grade teachers.)

Mike and Mary Anne are challenged to complete a dig in less than a day in the town of Popperville. Once the digging begins, we read Burton's onomatopoeia as her words match the sounds and motions of Mary Anne working at great speeds to meet the challenge. "Bing! Bang! Crash! Slam!" This reminded me of my mom and dad, who told me "not to hop in the house," and wear my leg or use my "sticks," or crutches. "A herd of elephants," is what Dad said I sounded like when hopping around. He warned me, "One of these days you're going to go through the floor!" The prosthesis made other noises, like Mary Anne's shovel. A screw-loose "click," a rubbing "squeak," a weight-bearing "clack," all combined in a magical, simple machine symphony.

Like the labeled parts of Mary Anne on the inside pages, it was also important for me to understand how things worked and to have labels, or definitions, for my human and machine parts. How my prosthesis stayed on, and how my prosthetist used machines and materials to make a comfortable socket were things I wanted, and needed, to know.

Back then, prosthetists would often tell my mom and me that I didn't need an artificial leg.

"He'd walk in a flower pot if we gave him one," I heard Mr. Williams say more than once.

That's where Mom got the idea. I remember her threatening to make a flower pot or a planter out of an old leg that I had outgrown. She and I did a lot of brainstorming about how to do it, but the foot always posed a problem, so we never made one.

Mike and Mary Anne do their jobs well. Too well, in fact, as they dig themselves a hole so deep they can't get out. A classic dilemma, and one we've all experienced as children and adults. I am not a golfer, but Mike Mulligan gets a mulligan, a do-over. He and his steam shovel get a second chance in Popperville.

The best authors engage our imaginations as we empathize and identify with their characters. I'm not Mike Mulligan, the little boy standing over the hole, or even Dickie Birkenbush, the author's neighbor credited in the book with the solution to the problem.

I'm Mary Anne! Don't let her name fool you. Mary Anne's a girl who loves to get dirty digging in the dirt. She's a boy's girl. The kind of girl who would go outside and join a game of pickle, ride a bike through the middle of a deep puddle, talk Red Sox baseball, or "play cars" using real Matchboxes in my imaginary town beside the driveway on Nanumet Drive.

Today, Burton's Mary Anne is an inspiration to readers and writers and an example of our human ingenuity. When people have something that no longer works as it was intended, it can be repurposed to make something new. It's called upcycling, but I like to think of it as a work of art, just like my favorite children's book, written in 1939.

I take Mary Anne down from the shelf every once in a while. Susan and I are child-free, but we still read children's books, often aloud, to each other. (*The Plot Chickens*, by Mary Jane and Herm Auch is the latest we recommend.) There is no higher praise for literature than putting it into new hands, so I gave the book to my coworker Laura to add to her baby's library. Rereading it again to write this review, I found some wonderful memories of Dad, Mom, Mary Anne, and myself. I'm continually amazed at how reading fills our imaginations, inspires learning, and shapes our identity no matter our age.

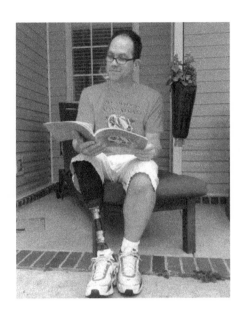

The Outing of My Leg

D. "The first thing I do is always the same; I pick up my pencil and write my name."

"The first thing I do to avoid the shame; I put on my prosthesis so I'm not lame."

In 1974, we lived on Nanumet Drive in Brewster. It's a strange land Dad called "a subdivision." The school bus picked me up at Prell Circle and Millstone Road for the trip to Brewster Elementary. There the school bus pulled into the long narrow driveway. The land in front of the school had a soccer field and two baseball fields. At the top of the hill was an old shingled building with a cupola on top.

Mrs. Gill wrote a letter to my parents that I "successfully completed" the first day of second grade. Later that year, I posed for our class picture, minus most of my front teeth, in front of the school with the flagpoles and fields behind us.

Every day we had a snack in the afternoon and if it was nice we'd go outside for recess. The door to the playground was on the south side of the school. In addition to hide and seek, tag, and "it," there were things to play on. We had swings, a slide, a merry-go-round, see-saws, monkey bars, and a jungle gym. The merry-go-round was in the middle of the playground in a pit of sand. When the sun was out, it hurt to grab onto the hot metal bars and it was tough to stand up on the sandy, slippery, metal decking. The rest of the playground was lined up along the property line and shaded under trees. The monkey bars always drew a crowd. It was the lure of monkey fights and one-on-one competition. In a page taken from the King of the Hill playbook, the winner always faced new challengers.

After waiting in line for half of recess, it was my turn to monkey fight. I climbed the two steps and jumped for the first rung. Hand-over-hand I went until my opponent was two or three bars away. I don't remember who moved first, but feet and legs were flailing. He got his legs higher than mine and was able to scissor onto my waist. I squirmed, wiggled, and lifted myself up trying to get out of his hold. His lock slipped down to my thighs. I thought I had a chance now if I could open my legs and break the hold. I felt a slight tug that I'd never felt before. My leg slid off and hit the ground. The kid stared down at my wooden leg on the ground. It took forever for the kid to drop his legs.

"Sorry," he said, as if he'd just ruined my life, and his own, in a schoolyard monkey fight. He never took his eyes off the leg on the ground—until he started wailing.

Seeing me hanging there, one kid in line yelled, "Get the nurse." I hung from the bars for what seemed forever.

"Did it get cut off?" No.

"Where's the blood?" I don't know.

"Is that a peg leg?" I don't think so. At the time, I really didn't know much more about my condition than the kids staring up at me. The voices changed from curious to critical, *and* mean.

"That's a wooden leg."

"He's a cripple!"

"Hey, Peg Leg." I had never been called these words before. They were attacking me with word arrows when I was completely defenseless, vulnerable. Once these words were flung there was no taking it back and the arrow hurts even more when you try to remove the sharpest, most painful insults. Even after they are removed, the emotional scars remain, and you begin to build your own defenses.

31

I looked down at the leg and tried to block out the yells and screams. For the first time, kids saw me without a leg. My empty right Toughskins' pant leg with the patch over the knee flapped in the fall breeze. The brown shiny wooden leg sat in the compacted dirt path below the bars. The jagged-edged broken leather strap let go just below the buckle that connected it to my waistband.

I was going to be in trouble for breaking it. Now Mom would have to take me all the way to Shriners Hospital for Crippled Children in Springfield to get it fixed.

"What happened to you?" A girl's voice found me above the noise.

"I was born like this," repeating something I heard my mother say but still didn't fully understand.

"That's my prroff prosssfff, fake leg," I said, looking down at the ground, still not able to wrap my tongue around the word prosthesis.

I'm not sure which was worse, the talk, or the fact that more people had gathered to stare at me, as if they'd heard about it through some playground news pipeline: "Go see the cripple hanging from the monkey bars!" My left foot was just two or three feet from the ground. I couldn't let go of the bar.

The principal, a burly man with wispy black hair, came out the front door and the kids suddenly stood quiet. I didn't see the nurse right away because she must have come from the side door.

"Let me help you down, Alan," Mr. Bridgewood said as he walked in front of me and held onto my wrists. "Let go of the bar," he said, and I felt my body land safely onto his back.

"Grab onto my neck," he said, and I wrapped my arms around his throat. When I looked down, the principal held my good leg from behind my knee as the nurse bent down to grab my fake leg. The kids stared at the leg outstretched in the nurse's hands.

As he piggy-backed me up the slight hill toward the front of the school, I held onto his neck and looked at my wooden leg. As the breeze fluttered the principal's tie, my tears began to roll.

Mom and I at the house in Brewster.

Shedding Our Shells

E. "The ocean thunders, pale wisps and windy tatters of wintry cloud sail over the dunes, and the sandpipers stand on one leg and dream."

If I promised to be careful, and not get my artificial leg wet, Ma would let me keep my leg on. That way, my sister Lynne and I could walk the sandy flats of Skaket and First Encounter Beach at low tide. Ma always made me keep a shoe on the prosthesis, so I must have looked a little strange walking the beach with one shoe on and one shoe off.

You really couldn't tell if the horseshoe crabs on the beach were dead just by looking at them. I remember the time Lynne picked up a crab by the tail to see if it was alive. We saw little tiny legs wiggling and waving. Seeing that it was still alive, Lynne put the tail back down. Sometimes we'd just see the shell with no tail. I learned later that the crabs lost their shells and grew bigger ones as they got older.

Lynne and I eventually wandered back to the dry sand and the beach towels.

"Ma, can we go in?" I asked. No matter what body of water we were near, the bay, the Atlantic, a pond, or even a swimming pool, I don't recall her ever saying no to a swim. Unless we'd just eaten, then we had to wait an hour. Just the thought of a swim in Cape Cod Bay lifted away the weight of the walking world. I knew that starfish grew their arms back, but I was more interested in shedding a false leg and hopping the rippled sand flats of Skaket Beach to reach the water.

I yanked on the Velcro of my waistband strap and pulled the fuzzy side through the metal buckle. With the tension slacked, I lifted my stump out of the prosthesis and took off my stump sock, and balanced on one foot.

Mom noticed I was limping more than usual, but now she saw something she didn't like.

"Sit down for a minute. Let me look at your leg."

"Lynne's waiting for me," I protested. At thirteen, she didn't need to wait for me, and was already wading in the bay, a half mile away.

"Cool your jets for a minute!" she snapped at my protest, and I plopped onto the sand. That summer, when I was nine, Mom knew I was wearing my leg less often because it hurt to walk in it. My bones were beginning to grow out of the end of my stump. My stump was fleshy with a full knee and a birth mark just above the outer part of my knee. "My dirt mark" I used to call it. Behind my knee was a speed bump of fat. The roll stretched the entire length of the back of my knee and would not fit inside the socket of my prosthesis. It hung over the socket like my father's belly hung over his pants.

I can't remember the name I had for my birth defect, but I often talked to it like a character on *Sesame Street*. I held it up, aimed and fired it like a pistol. Pekow! I flexed my knee so fast that I thought the flubbering fat was falling off the bone because I felt pulses in new places.

I remember pulling extra skin over the end of my stump and hiding my toes. My five toes were little fatty nubs of skin on the end that looked like the soft tips of real toes.

The toes were sunburn red that day, and sore.

"You have an appointment at Shriners soon," she said. She softened her tone, like she knew something I didn't.

"I know, Ma," but she kept staring at my stump, which she never did. I saw a worried look on her face, but I didn't know why she was worried.

"I'm goin' in, okay?" I said, and sprung into my three-point stance, before bouncing up on one foot.

"Yeah, the salt water's good for it," Ma said.

Balancing on one foot for a second, I bounded down the soft sand, onto a flat, and flopped into a foot-and-a-half deep tidal pool. Salty wet, I got back on one foot and raced like I was readying for a fifty-yard dash. It was a long hop.

I rested next to an abandoned shell from a horseshoe crab, the brown prehistoric sand-slogging shellfish with the long tail. The horseshoe crab and I were brothers of the bay. As we grew up, we left our exoskeletal shells on the sand, and floated away on the rising tide.

SHRINERS HOSPITAL FOR CRIPPLED CHILDREN
516 CAREW STREET, SPRINGFIELD, MASS. TEL: 781-6750

NAME: Samry, Alan   UNIT #: 11176

RETURN: JAN 14, 1977
           Apr - 8 · 1977
           MAY - 25-1977
           Aug - 12 1977

WEDNESDAY AND THURSDAY CLINICS 8 to 11
TO KEEP APPOINTMENT PLEASE NOTIFY THE HOSPITAL

SHRINERS HOSPITAL FOR CRIPPLED CHILDREN
516 CAREW STREET, SPRINGFIELD, MASS. TEL: 781-675

NAME: Alan Samry   UNIT # 11176

RETURN: October 28, 1977
           Feb 24, 1978
           June 23, 1978

WEDNESDAY & THURSDAY CLINICS 8 to 11 A.M.
IF UNABLE TO KEEP APPOINTMENT PLEASE NOTIFY THE HOSPITAL

Copy-Amputation

SHRINERS HOSPITAL FOR CRIPPLED CHILDREN   SPRINGFIELD   Unit

Admission Date ___8-15-77___ Discharge Date ___8-27-77___ Age ___9⁸___ Sex ___M___

FINAL DIAGNOSIS:

    Transverse deficiency right lower leg.

CHIEF COMPLAINT AND ESSENTIAL PHYSICAL FINDINGS:

  This is the first Shriners' Hospital admission for this 9 yr. 8 month old male who has been followed here since July, 68' for transverse deficiency of the right leg. The reason he is admitted is for spiking and overgrowth of the tibia and fibula at the stump site aswell as overall varus deformity and prominence of the fibular head. This had resulted in poor prosthetic fitting, irritation over the end of the stump and antalgic gait culminating in patient's inability to use the prosthesis.

PHYSICAL EXAM: Within normal limits except for evidence spiking and varus deformity. X-rays showed a fusion distally between the fibula and tibia.

COURSE IN THE HOSPITAL:

  The patient was presented to conference. Discussion between doing high coventry type osteotomy and then revision of stump was discuessed. However, on 8-17-77 the patient underwent a revision of stump on the right leg with resection ofaproximately 1½" of the distal tibia and fibula and a modified Ertl procedure. The patient was placed in rigid dressing. Postop the patient did well and on 8-24-77 a rigid dressing was removed, the wound was inspected and found to be fine and a new rigid dressing was applied. The patient was up with physical therapy & the decision was made by Dr. Kruger to discharge the patient home to await fitting with the prosthesis.

Name—Last	First	Middle	Hospital No.
SAMSY,	ALAN		11176

Form 1023   SUMMARY   PRINTED IN U.S.A.

SHRINERS HOSPITAL FOR CRIPPLED CHILDREN   SPRINGFIELD   Unit

Surgeon __Dr. Reitman__   First Assistant __Dr. Kruger__

Second Assistant ____   Third Assistant ____

Surgical Nurse __Mrs. Jane Markham, R.N.__   Circulating Nurse __Mrs. Joann Gemelli, R.N.__

Sponge Count ____   Drains ____   Packs ____

Anesthetic __Dr. Chakrabarti-General.__

Date __8-17-77__ Operation Began __4:40 p.m.__ a.m./p.m. Operation Ended __4:55 p.m.__ a.m./p.m.

PREOPERATIVE DIAGNOSIS: Transverse deficiency left leg with Overgrowth ("spiking") at stump. Varus deformity.

POSTOP DIAGNOSIS: Same.

(Modified Ertl)

OPERATION: Stump revision and application of rigid dressing, left leg.

PROCEDURE: The patient successfully underwent general anesthesia. The right lower extremity was sterilely scrubbed and draped. The lower extremity was examined and the distal end of tibia and fibula were seen to be protruding at the distal end of the stump. The overall lower extremity below the knee had a varus added to it with moderate bowing of tibia and fibula. There was dimpling of the skin distally. A curvey linear incision was made over the distal end of the stump extending medially from approximately 3 finger breadths both medially and laterally. Incision was carried down through skin and subcutaneous tissue. An elliptical area including the dimpled skin distally was excised, thus, providing two generous flaps of soft tissue. Incision was carried directly down through skin subcutaneous tissue fascia and periosteum. The shaft of the bone was thus exposed through periosteal elevation. A longitudinal osteotomy was made at the distal spike of the bone. It should be noted that the fibula and tibia were synostosed, that is, fused distally, solidly, for an area of at least 3 finger breadths. A longitudinal osteotomy was made preserving the posterolateral portion of bone, attached to soft tissue. A transverse saw cut was then made through the distal end of the stump resecting approximately 1 ½" of bone. The longitudinal portion excluded from the transverse osteotomy which remained attached to the soft tissue to was then Green-Sticked and bent across the transverse osteotomy site thus "capping" the distally revised stump. This was easily held in the reduced position. The deep soft tissue, that is, periosteum and fascial was repaired in interrupted fashion using heavy chromic catgut suture in figure of 8 fashion. The more superficial fascia was closed in interrupted fashion using chromic catgut suture. The subcutaneous tissue was closed in interrupted fashion using plain catgut suture. The skin was closed in interrupted fashion using nylon catgut and nylon suture. A superficial running skin stitch was then used over the interrupted skin sutures. A dry sterile dressing followed by application of a well-padded, well-molded, rigid compression dressing was then applied. Stump sock, felt, belt, were all employed. The knee was left approximately 7° of flexion

Pneumatic tourniquet was employed and tourniquet time was less than 30 minutes. The patient tolerated the procedure well and was brought to the recovery room in good condition. Signature of Surgeon _____ (Dr. Reitman)

D&T: 8-17-77

ORDER OF RECORDING
1. Diagnosis - Preoperative
2. Diagnosis - Postoperative
3. Procedure
4. Operation & Findings
5. Signature

Name—Last __SAMRY,__   First __ALAN__   Middle ____   Hospital No. __11176__

Form 1004   OPERATION RECORD   Dr. Kruger

2. Teens

F. "Sometimes one who thinks himself incomplete is merely young."

Fall of the film spool pyramid with David Heath.
Falmouth High School Class of 1985 Yearbook

Key Largo

Bobbing in liquid turquoise
I float over the coral reef and see
my three-and-a-half-limbed shadow
swimming on a stretch of sandy bottom

Fire Starters

G. "Each of us is more than the worst thing we've ever
done."

Responsibility for the 1871 fire that burned more than
14,000 buildings and left 100,000 homeless in Chicago is now
being laid at the foot of an amputee and not Mrs. O'Leary's
cow.

I had requested this book—*The Great Chicago Fire and the
Myth of Mrs. O'Leary's Cow*, by Richard Bale (Jefferson, NY:
McFarland and Company, Inc. 2002)—through an interlibrary
loan after reading a review on Amazon that said the book,
written by a title insurance adjuster, was full of detail, but "very
dull." It used details from the Chicago Board of Police and Fire
Commissioners Investigation transcripts and title maps to come
up with a new guilty party. In 1997, 126 years after the fire, the
Chicago City Council's Committee on Fire and Police
exonerated Mrs. O'Leary and her cow.

"Mrs. Kate O'Leary and her cow are innocent of any blame
for the fire that raged behind their house," Alderman Ed Burke
is quoted in the *Chicago Tribune* article. Based on Bale's
research, Burke and others began mounting the case against
Daniel "Peg Leg" Sullivan for starting the fire.

No actions or votes were taken to pin the fire on Sullivan,
but I was curious about whether this four-hundred-page book
with lots of great illustrations would change my perception
about who started the fire when public opinion through
newspaper accounts had for so long pinned the cause on a cow.
Did Peg Leg Sullivan really start the fire?

In the final 1871 report of the investigation of the fire, the
commissioners wrote, "The fire was first discovered by a

drayman by the name of Daniel Sullivan, who saw it while sitting on the sidewalk, on the south side of DeKoven Street, and nearly opposite Leary's premises."

On November 25th, Sullivan gave his testimony to city officials in charge of determining the cause of the October 8th fire. Sullivan went to the O'Learys' after work, and then went to a party at the house next to the O'Learys'. He went outside after 9 PM and sat on the sidewalk across the street. As he was getting up to go home, Sullivan stated, "I saw a fire in O'Leary's barn. I got up and run across the street and kept hollering, 'fire, fire, fire.'" Seeing the fire coming through the side of the barn, he ran down an alley north of the O'Leary property. On account of his peg, he said, "I couldn't run very quick." His first instinct was to rescue the livestock, the horses and cows in the barn. He managed to get two cows loose, then testified that, "the place was too hot" and he headed for the barn door. "The boards were wet and my legs slipped out from me and I went down." When he got to the door, "There was a Goddamned big calf come along, and the back of the calf was all afire, and Christ, I thought it was time I got out." Once at a safe distance Sullivan testified, "The calf was all burnt. I stood and looked back at the fire as a dog will look when he is licked with a rope."

The book cover shows Mrs. O'Leary's cow kicking over the lamp with her hind leg, igniting the hay on the barn floor. An illustration inside the book shows how the fire might have been started by Sullivan. It shows Sullivan and another man, Dennis Regan, smoking in the O'Leary barn. Regan is sitting on the floor next to a knocked over and presumably empty whiskey bottle. With the floor visibly wet, Sullivan is tripping on his peg leg and his pipe is falling into some fresh wood shavings. After looking at the image of Sullivan, mouth open, his hat floating above his head as he falls to the floor, I thought about my own history with fire on Cape Cod.

***

Eric and I started burning clumps of weeds just up the hill from the pump house that grabs water from Mill Pond to water the two cranberry bogs south of Old Barnstable Road in East Falmouth. The green lighter from Cumberland Farms was clear enough to see how much fuel was in each of the two reservoirs. We were 13, high, and drunk. It was one of those days a couple of years before our friend, George Crocker, drowned in the very same sandy-bermed channel near the pump house in 1983. The grass was bright spring green in some places and still dead brown in others. The fire started small. Eric and I would alternate cupping hands and lighting the grass. We'd light a clump and watch it burn. The dry grass hissed and crackled, and the flames danced a foot off the ground, and then it would quickly die. So, we'd light two clumps at a time and then step on them before they died. Suddenly, we realized we had lit too much weed!

We panicked as the wind took the fire. Clump to clump. Tuft to tuft. It went up the hill with a mind of its own, obeying a south wind sweeping off Vineyard Sound three miles away. I had a leg back then that was plastic, not wood, probably with a Seattle Foot and a P-Lite Liner. I stepped on the clumps with my good leg while balancing on my prosthesis. I was scared and I'm pretty sure Eric, who was stomping around in his work boots, was scared too. We began whumping it with our coats. The coat I had was all black and felt kind of rubbery. When I looked down I noticed my sneaker tread had melted from the heat. Eric always wore a blue jean jacket and he was managing to snuff out some of the flames. We were no match for the wind, though, which seemed to strengthen, change direction and push the fire into the tree line. We didn't run. I don't know if we thought we could contain the fire, but I think I started yelling "fire" at some point, hoping someone would call 911. Eventually, someone did.

As the leaves, branches, and weeds hissed and moaned I heard the faint whir of the fire truck siren. It was coming from the station practically in my back yard off Fortaleza Drive, less than a mile away by foot. As I fought the blaze downwind, I looked up to see the flames widen and lengthen as they burned their way up the hill toward a small white house. The fire department arrived. We couldn't see the truck from where we were standing, but by then other people had come to help us whack down the flames with whatever they had. I saw the water sizzle out the flames before I ever spotted a fireman. They put out the fire just a few yards from the propane tank in the back yard of the white vinyl-sided ranch.

Clouds had moved in by the time the fire was under control. The fireman in charge looked at us (we were ashen-faced) and knew we'd caused the fire.

"What happened?" he asked us. Eric or I put a lie on the fire. One of us told the fireman that the fire was already burning.

"We tried to put it out," we repeated. At first I was looking down at the singed black tree trunks. By then the tears had dried, leaving Eric and me with soot-streaked faces. I remember looking up at the unfurling leaves on the large white oaks. Someone caught the fireman's attention and Eric and I walked quickly down the hill past the scene of the crime.

***

A century after the Chicago fire, author Richard Bales used a lot of illustrations, diagrams, maps, title records, newspaper accounts, and the testimony of the Police and Fire Commission to prove it was Sullivan. "There is circumstantial evidence that Sullivan lied," Bale told *People Magazine* in 1997. Bale believed that Sullivan could not have seen the fire from the sidewalk because a two-story house would have blocked Sullivan's view of the barn.

The official 1871 report of the Chicago Fire concluded that, "Whether it originated from a spark blown from a chimney on that windy night or was set on fire by human agency, we are unable to determine." The story of Mrs. O'Leary's cow starting the fire appeared in the October 9 issue of the *Chicago Evening Journal*. The Extra edition reports the start of the fire was "caused by a cow kicking over a lamp in the stable in which a woman was milking."

Despite Bale's book, and the action by the Chicago City Council exonerating Mrs. O'Leary, the O'Leary cow story is safe from being supplanted by the alleged actions of Daniel Sullivan, at least in the popular imagination.

The cow starting the fire has become legend and my own history with fire hit closer to home than I ever expected. In 1992, my wife, Susan, and I moved into our first house on Prince Henry Drive in Falmouth. After a few months, the sloping backyard and mature oak trees became eerily familiar. As I looked up at the house from the backyard, I realized that we had bought the house Eric and I nearly burned down. We lived in the house for thirteen years.

The only record of my fire is perhaps a mention in the fire logs of the *Falmouth Enterprise*. Since no personal property was damaged, the fire may not have appeared anywhere. Ten years after the Chicago fire, Sullivan lived on DeKoven Street and continued to deliver coal and oil as a drayman.

The fires occurred in different centuries, but Sullivan and I share a few similarities. We both yelled "fire," tried to put it out, gave the authorities accounts of our actions, and remained in the neighborhood for years afterward. Even though Eric and I were first on the scene, no one ever asked if I started the fire. In his own testimony, Sullivan admits to being first on the scene, but no one ever asked Sullivan if he started the fire either. Maybe the cause didn't matter as much as our actions. While wearing artificial legs, Sullivan and I both held our feet to the fire.

Three Legs of a Bedroom Life

> H. "Hazel Grace," he said, "do you have a pen and a piece
> of paper?" I said I did. "Okay, please draw a circle." I
> did. "Now draw a smaller circle within that circle." I
> did. "The larger circle is virgins. The smaller circle is
> seventeen-year-old guys with one leg."

You wake up every morning and it's leaning next to your bed. Today, you're fourteen and your supra-condylar below-the-knee exoskeletal patella tendon-bearing right leg prosthesis is two. You pick up your leg so you can put it on and you get a whiff of your "eau de funk." It's like a sweat sock that's been in the bottom of the dirty clothes pile for a month. It should have odor trails like a Pepé Le Pew cartoon.

Exoskeletal means that the metal shaft and foot is encased by either a hard or soft outside cover. The solid covering of your leg is a brown fiberglass shell that does not look like a real leg at all. The large calf area is made to match the shape of your overdeveloped "good leg." It has a plastic, shiny coating, with scratches. There are knife holes in varying sizes from friends with Buck knives and kitchen knives stabbing you in the leg to scare or amuse strangers. Your foot is a hunk of carved beige rubber shaped like a surfboard.

You know the phrase "congenital defect," but you dwell on the latter word as you have understood for a long time that your deformity came "from birth." Your four brothers and sisters and your parents have told you that your birth was an "accident" because you were not "planned," and that further complicates the phrase.

Your leg is made at Shriners Hospital for Crippled Children, where you have been a patient since you were a year old. From

East Falmouth, the hospital is a three-hour drive away in Springfield, Massachusetts. You have already had two surgeries and you know there will be more. You used to have toes too, but you never had a foot and the toes just looked like different sized lumps on the distal end of your flabby stump. Those toes, along with a bulbous fibula head, were removed along with about two inches of your tibia so you could have a leg that fit properly.

You are humbled at Shriners Hospital because you see other kids missing parts of all four limbs. There is no wallowing in self-pity. Everything is free at Shriners. Yes, free, and you will never know how much it all costs. You thank them by walking, riding a bike, and running with reckless abandon.

You have already lived in this leg a year longer than you will live in this house on Winchester Drive. Your bedroom will forever be remembered as the one your drunken dad came into that night and pissed in the corner. You cleaned it up. The sweaty leg and urine brought you to your knees in tears.

After you wake in the morning, you put on a few five-ply Knit Rite socks. You insert your stump into the liner made of quarter-inch thick Pelite, a foam rubber material. It acts as a buffer between your leg and the hard plastic/fiberglass socket that the liner fits into. Both the socket and the liner are smooth and contour to the shape of your stump, except for the indent or bar that sticks out below your knee that bears your body weight on the patella tendon. The Pelite liner has thick wedges on the left and right sides that rest over the condyles of the femur, hence the name supra-condylar. If you grab the sides of your leg above your knee and push down, those are the condyles of your femur. You then insert your stump with the Pelite liner into the socket of the prosthesis, and the supra-condylar wedges lock you into the socket to keep the prosthesis on your stump.

The leg grabs onto the inner condyle so tight that the bone pain from the day before returns. The two-inch-wide leather Y strap attaches to the outside of the socket and you wrap it around your waist over your underwear, which helps reduce the beltline marks on your skin. The strap is there for added suspension because, as you go through the day, your stump shrinks and swells, and friction is the worst thing for any prosthesis wearer because it leads to sores. The strap is also your woobie because you have always had one and it makes you feel secure.

***

It was the early eighties and years before condoms would be available at our high school (one of the first in the nation to dispense rubbers from vending machines in the bathrooms). Katie and I had similar hairdos. My brown straight hair parted in the middle and dangled at the top of my shoulders, covering what I thought were my enormous ears. I looked like Scooby's best friend Shaggy. The ends of Katie's hair, which was golden and more yellow than blonde, curled into the middle of her back. I had a long face with a smirk on it. She had a Bugs Bunny smile. We had moles above our lips in mirror images of one another. It was springtime; she was a sophomore and I was a freshman.

Katie's dad owned a laundromat and dry-cleaning store, and he had a few video games near the dry-cleaning pickup and drop-off counter. On weekends she used to watch me play video games for a while, and then we'd go into the little back room to explore each other over and under our fully clothed bodies. She seemed to enjoy it when I used my fingers inside her, but she also liked it when I rubbed that bump at the top of her opening. Like the fire button on my favorite video game,

Defender, I kept pressing it faster to go further in the game with Katie.

When her parents went away in April, we cut class and had a party at her house. We drank Tuborg beer and she smoked cigarettes in the kitchen. Then we smoked some of her brother's home-grown with him. This latest batch was offered from a large wooden salad bowl. It looked more like spinach, wet, leafy, and dark green, not like anything we ever paid for or saw in *Cheech and Chong* movies.

Their house was a mess. Dirty dishes, stuff piled in corners. Her bedroom was the same way, but the room was dark and smelled like Katie: a blend of sweat, Johnson's baby powder, and Prell shampoo. She pushed some dirty clothes from the unmade twin bed onto the floor and we sat down and started kissing. She reached inside my underwear and gave me a hand job. I fidgeted with the bra strap on her back until she eventually undid it for me. Katie took off the bra through her shirt sleeves and we took off our pants and our tighty-whities. I pulled her shirt up over her breasts; I don't remember how I got my underwear off because I never undid my suspension strap.

We could not lie flat on the bed because of all the clothes and the covers, so Katie was in kind of curled caterpillar position when I moved on top of her. We tried for a while with my prosthesis on, but the metal buckle was digging into her belly. I sensed her discomfort, but I'd realize later it was from my inability to perform and not from the buckle.

"Why don't you take it off?" she whispered.

"Are you sure?" I did not want to. We had gotten to this point with most of our clothing still on because we were self-conscious about our bodies. During our sneaky sexual adventures our hands had touched all the intimate areas, but until today we had never laid eyes on those places. She had never seen me with my leg off and I had never glimpsed the places my hands knew so well. I pressed down on the toe of the prosthetic leg with my left foot to hold it down as I pulled my stump out. With a little more foreplay, we repositioned ourselves. I was on top of her and my hardness suddenly softened. I remember Katie pulling my hips into hers, still not wanting to give up. I wished I had one of those strap-on models like I'd seen in a catalogue. I was used to putting on prosthetics and would have gladly strapped it on just to see the passionate colors of pleasure light up Katie's face.

Days later, a group of us were walking together to the cleaners to play video games. Katie's and my relationship was already different—tense and distant—and it was not going to improve. We made some mean comments to each other and it escalated into personal attacks along the way. I don't remember what she said, but my vicious response was the product of some heightened teen pack mentality.

"You're a fuckin'....!" I yelled.

"You can't get it up!" She shouted to me, her face an angry flame.

"Limp dick!" She shouted it while crossing the street so all our friends and the people in the cars stopped at the traffic light on Route 28 could hear. With my friend Andy beside me, I stood there stunned and hurt by her anger, but the truth and shame knotted my stomach. She walked in the other direction with her friend and her brother Mike.

Katie and I never spoke to each other again. We lived less than two miles from each other for nearly two decades.

Still angry and embarrassed by what Katie said, I stopped with Andy at a flowering bush with yellow jackets flying around it. We loved to capture the bees in the cups of our hands. Today, I shook them up in my hands for a few seconds and felt them bounce off my palms and fingers, daring them to sting.

Some days we would fling our hands open in a throwing motion and the bees would fly away buzzing mad. Sometimes they would drop toward the ground in silent dizziness and then restart their buzzing engines before ever hitting the ground. I opened my hands and the bee flew away in a spiral up into the trees.

The bees always lived and I never got stung.

***

You look at the relic of a leg leaning on the wall. You just turned sixteen and your exoskeletal below-the-knee joints and corset patella tendon-bearing prosthesis has been around since the American Civil War. James Hanger opened one of the first prosthetic leg businesses in the United States in 1861 for Civil War veterans, and your late 20th-century version could have passed as his floor model.

You live two houses away from Winchester Drive on Edgewater Drive West, but your home is far from the water's edge. Your bedroom is remembered for the white walls stained yellow by chain smoking parents. You are in the smallest bedroom because you had to move when your two sisters had babies and the four of them had nowhere else to go. Seven people in a three-bedroom ranch with one bathroom. It's the only time you have nightmares. After major surgery to remove a pie-shaped wedge from your tibia, the same dream of being eaten limb by limb by a tiger haunts you for many nights. It could be the drugs for the pain, but you know it's rooted deep in your psyche and will manifest itself in other ways once the pain is gone.

You put on a wool sock and slide the stump through the leather brace with the corset untied until it rests in the Pelite liner that stays in the socket. You pull the laces of the corset, which are made out of parachute cord, and then tie it at the top of your thigh just under the condyles at the top of the femur. This corset bears all your weight and is supported by joints, two large metal hinges on the sides of the corset that attach to the lower part of the leg socket. The leg is held on by a Y-shaped suspension strap because without it the leg would slide off, no matter how tight you tied the corset. You have no lateral knee movement at all and the hinges of the joints shred every pair of pants you own. You never have any sores on your stump and the leg is very secure.

The problem with the old joints and corset, or thigh lacer, is that your leg muscles atrophy from not being used and your puny-sized thigh gets even smaller. Occasionally, your mouth dries out and you hyperventilate in pain when your nut gets pinched between the corset and your thigh. The new Seattle foot actually looks real with veins and it even has five little rubber toes on the end. This energy-storing foot is made of a new plastic developed by DuPont, literally giving you a spring in your step.

***

Cindy had long, light brown hair and the personality of a tiger cub—playful, mischievous and constantly moving. She had an oval face with pouty lips I thought were the result of the braces on her teeth. She had carefree blue eyes. Cindy was a new wave and pop freshman and I was a serious head banging senior tuning out to Metallica, Dio, and Motley Crue. We had nothing in common except that I was attracted to her slim body.

It was winter, and we were at my sister's apartment downtown on King Street. Her place was an old farmhouse chopped up and added onto so that it now contained four apartments. By late afternoon, there were flurries flying outside the two east-facing windows above my sister's double bed. Cindy and I were holding each other, kissing, and taking off articles of clothing. Suddenly there was nothing left to take off.

"Are you warm enough?" I asked. Cindy nodded and as our eyes met, we laughed, nervously. She lay down on top of the flowered bedspread.

Time moves a lot faster when you're naked. I wanted to slow time down to study her body with all my senses. Cindy was a still life work of art; unmoving, with arms at her sides and legs together. Her limbs were long and smooth. I remember feeling her skin, quivering sometimes at my touch. She got goose bumps. I kissed her all over. I licked the fuzz below her navel and it tasted salty. She smelled like fresh baked bread and I tasted a girl for the first time. With her hips rising up to meet my lips, I was pleased that she was pleased.

"I'm ready," she whispered. Damn! I told myself I would take my leg off this time and I got so caught up in our intimacy that I had forgotten. Unstrap. Unlace. De-leg.

"I'm ready," she whispered over and over into my ear. I was not. And as I lay down beside her, ashamed to even look in her direction, I questioned if I ever would be. I put my underwear on and Cindy got dressed and left.

Cindy and I drifted apart, and later that year she moved away. Cindy was willing to accept me for what I was and I didn't understand that. I wasn't willing to accept me for who I was. She called my mother's house a few years later asking for me, but by then I was already engaged to Susan.

***

I've just turned forty and the latest leg, an endoskeletal below-the-knee silicone suction socket (3-S) prosthesis leans against Susan's nana's chair. There is no cover on this leg, it's endoskeletal and has a carbon fiber post. The post is attached with titanium hardware to the carbon fiber socket on one end and the foot on the other. In this case, it's a Freedom Innovations Renegade foot with Z-shock technology. Our bedroom has the bureaus that match the chair and Grandma Samry's rocking chair is in the other corner of our new Fairhope, Alabama, home.

First, I apply the petroleum-based cream to lubricate my stump, now called the residual limb for political correctness. Then I put on a silicone gel liner over my stump, which covers my kneecap. A precursor of the silicone gel system came out in the late eighties, but the technology would not take off commercially until ten years later. I put on a nylon sock so the gel liner does not stick to the carbon fiber. I stand up and my weight drops into the socket, making farting noises as the excess air escapes out of the top of the gel liner, which feels like hard Jell-O. As I put the leg on, I laugh out loud at the old adage about everyone putting on their pants one leg at a time. I grab the Flexisport polyethylene suspension sleeve, which is made of a rubber-like material and grips onto the carbon fiber socket. I roll the Flexisport sleeve over my thigh and the outside material feels like a wetsuit. This system is the best socket liner system, hands down. Then I put my pants on. I only change one sock every day, unless the color changes. My right sock never gets dirty.

I feel guilty about the fact that the reason the technology is improving, like my new foot, is because of Improvised Explosive Devices. IEDs are separating limbs from soldiers in Iraq and sending them back home to their families "broken." The soldiers I've met are actually demanding better technology so they can maintain their active lifestyles. I've never demanded anything. I try not to take the ability to walk for granted and appreciate every step I have taken in a prosthesis.

After a typical day of wearing this thing for sixteen hours, I sit down on the edge of the bed, roll down the suspension sleeve onto the socket, lift my stump out of the socket, and push my fingers into the gel liner to "pop" myself out of the seal.

I've been putting on a leg when I wake up for about 14,000 days now. I have no idea how many consecutive days I have woken up and put my leg on. I'm too superstitious to even think about a streak. Sometimes you take it for granted, like putting on your socks. Many days it is a painful reminder that you are incomplete, in pain on every heel strike, and totally dependent on "durable medical equipment" just to take a step. I lean the leg on the chair, which has been a stand for the everyday leg, and the spare, for as long as I can remember.

***

It's October 2007, and I'm crutching out of the bathroom after getting ready for bed.

"I can't believe you just passed him without petting him. That's why he jumps up there," Sue says to me in her "you should feel guilty" tone. As I look at Sue, she cracks a mischievous smile and her brown eyes brighten. I turn to Jake, our indoor tubby tiger cat who is crouched on the edge of the bathtub. Jake has figured out that I can't bend over to pet him when I'm limbless and on crutches, so he has learned to jump up and sit on the side of the tub when I walk by.

"Sorry, buddy," I apologize and rub him under his chin and along his jaw line. I purr and so does he. Outside the bathroom, he runs in fear from the crutches.

Truth is, I'm afraid of the damn crutches too. One fall and my hip could be broken faster than you can say "I've fallen and I can't get up!" Much of this is due to "overuse syndrome," which means that my healthy side ages much faster because I'm overusing it. I used to be able to wield a glass of milk, a plate of food, utensils, and a napkin while crutching anywhere in my home. Too risky now that my body is actually sixty years old in some places, so I keep my hands on the grips. Also gone are the days of standing on one leg to take a shower.

Tonight, I turn out the light, sit on the bed and lean the crutches on the headboard. I lie down beside Sue in her T-shirt and underwear with her knees up in the air. She moves her fingers across the bumps and the deep red lines left behind by the suspension sleeve. I wrap my stump around the top of her upper thigh and begin running my fingers through her hair.

3. Nonfiction

I. "He writes of a tribe called the Monocoli who have only one leg and hop with amazing speed. The people are also called Umbrella footed, because when the weather is hot they lie on their backs stretched on the ground and protect themselves by the shade of their feet."

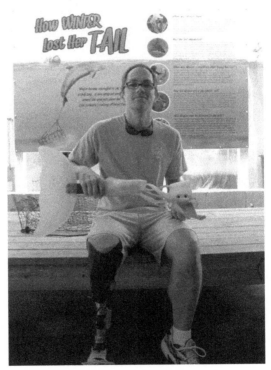

The leg I'm holding, at the Clearwater Florida Aquarium, was Winter the Dolphin's 17th prosthesis. The leg I'm wearing is state-of-the-art. It has a V-Hold electronic vacuum system. I was so excited to show off this new leg that I took my pants off to show the library director in the middle of the library! The library was closed at the time, of course.

My Native American Brother

J. "The one-legged man shot an arrow."

Sinewy skin smeared in bear grease to hold in my heat, my face, melancholy and dark, with lines aiming down from my ever-present frown. Beothuk, barefoot in the cold, in browns and reds I blend with the trees, standing tall and proud before strangers, admiring the black peat, green grass, and crystal blue icebergs drifting in the same current that will take my boat to hunting places. We are hunter gatherers padding on one foot yet silent as the lone branch swaying in a swift breeze.

The wind lashes my black hair against my bronze skin streaked with red dye. The deep blue sea has bright whitecaps. A whale breaches the surface. Slippery black, the dorsal fin waves at me. A beige square enters my brown eyes from beyond a spit of land. Paddles, powered by hairy creatures, dip into the water from a boat. This strange fur flies above the boat. It moves with the wind. "Oh, Creator! Sun, Sky, Water, and Wind." The same gust carries their putrid scent. I hop closer to see they are not me. The beasts beach their boat and lower the wind-taker. They make noises I do not understand and break the silence of Creator's breathing. They see me. They wear furs and skins, like I do, though mine are rusty red. My bow is always in my hand. I draw arrow, aim bow, and let go. A man with white hair bleeds red. The sun hides from me. The wind-takers shove off. These beasts row hard following the shoreline and pass in and out of my sight.

The large fur unfurls and the beasts take the wind.

Unipeds

The one-legged history of America can be traced all the way back to the Vikings at the turn of the first millennium, around the year 1000 AD. The North Atlantic Vikings, unlike their European counterparts, sought expansion away from Greenland to settle as farmers or craftsmen. Scholars actually agree that the Vikings succeeded in establishing a location on the North American continent where the first Europeans met Natives. Much of what we know today of Viking exploration comes from *The Greenland Saga* and *Erik the Red's Saga*. The sagas, or sayings, are written accounts, not by eyewitnesses, but transcriptions from oral traditions and are often contradictory. The sagas are comprised of two different works that were written down in Iceland in the early 13th century.

Leif Eriksson, whose father was Erik the Red, landed on the North American continent between 997 and 1003. Radio carbon dating of a Viking village at L'Anse aux Meadows on Épaves Bay in Northern Newfoundland confirmed information in the saga that the site was active between 980-1020. The sagas have been recognized as real sources of information and have led to the discovery of remains from the Viking age, but as with any oral tradition the sagas do not tell the full truth. They are a mixture of fact and fiction, and therefore do not belong in the same category as myths or legends.

The section pertaining to a one-legged creature is mentioned in *Erik the Red's Saga*, which deals predominantly with Gudrid Thorbjarnadottir and her husband Thorfinn Karlsefni on their journey from Greenland to Vinland (wine land), which had been named by Leif for the wild grapevines that grew.

"One morning Karlsefni's men saw something shiny above a clearing in the trees, and they called out. It moved and proved to be a one-legged creature which darted down to where the ship lay tied. Thorvald, Erik the Red's son, was at the helm and the one-legged man shot an arrow into his intestines. Thorvald drew the arrow and spoke: "Fat paunch that was. We've found a land of fine resources, though we'll hardly enjoy much of them." Thorvald died from the wound shortly after...They soon headed northward where they thought they sighted the Land of the One-Legged but did not want to put their lives in further danger." (Fitzhugh 224)

Thousands of books and articles discuss, speculate, hypothesize and attempt to uncover Viking activity in America. Thorvald's murder and later attacks by the hostile natives and their deadly accurate arrows and large populations were a major factor in the Viking retreat back to Greenland and Iceland. Yet there is little analysis, insight or investigation into the one-legged man of Vinland. What could be found traced the one-legged thing, in some translations called a "uniped," to an African or Indian Tribe in mythology. A uniped is defined as a creature with one foot, as compared to most humans who are classified as bipeds. It's difficult to picture a uniped as this is not a man with two legs and part of one missing. It's actually a person with the anatomy of one leg. Compare a uniped with the players on a foosball table, or a mermaid, minus her caudal fin. The African uniped apparently has a foot large enough to shield his whole body from the sun.

Why do scholars continue to use mythology to explain the one-legged creature when there is science to indicate that human deformity can be traced back much farther than mythology? It was probably a one-legged Native who shot Leif's brother Thorvald. Let's consider that the translation first referred to a creature, and then in the second reference called it a man. Skraeling, a derogatory word used by the Norsemen for Natives, was not used to refer to the one-legged being. Why? It was likely that he was perceived as a mythical figure by the Vikings, because of his deformity. This is perfectly suitable for their time as these explorers would have been familiar with the mythical belief of a uniped tribe. Approximately five hundred years later, French explorer Jacques Cartier reported a land peopled by unipeds in North America.

Was this one-legged man a uniped or a biped missing part of his leg, or was he a normal skraeling born of myth, created by the orators or the writers to glorify Thorvald's death? Let's consider that the uniped exists only in myth, but deformed human bodies can be traced back thousands of years before the Viking age. Deformity, whether occurring naturally or inflicted on humans to appease the gods or the result of war can be traced back tens of thousands of years ago. Evidence of our understanding of deformity relies on modern day anthropologists, who have evidence from 45,000 years ago that indicates an upper extremity amputee. Additional field work has uncovered cave paintings in France and Spain from 36,000 years ago that show a mutilated hand. Since no unipeds have ever been found, science, specifically anthropology, continues to find evidence that human malformations preceded man's creation of mythical monsters. It's time for scholars to debunk the myth. Karlsefni's men saw the first one-legged Native American.

Actual Peg-Legged Pirates

When you open up Jan Rogozinski's book *Pirates*, it seems fitting that parrots and peg legs are listed on opposite pages because both are mostly the stuff of legend from 19th century fiction writers. The one-legged pirate and the parrot have become falsely synonymous with pirates, most notably due to Robert Louis Stevenson's *Treasure Island*. The novel is a tremendous adventure and still holds up nicely today, but its crutch wielding one-legged pirate Long John Silver and his parrot were romanticized accounts written for younger audiences. It failed to show how murderous, selfish, and bloody a pirate's life could be.

As with limb loss, pirate reality and pirate fiction are not one and the same. The word "pirate" requires further explanation upon its impact in the Americas. Pirates are seamen who robbed others; and these sea raiders have been around since the 14th century BC, and established footholds along trade routes. When Columbus discovered the Bahamas in 1492, it marked the beginning of Spanish Colonial expansion that would ultimately control the entire New World. It also opened that same world to the expansion of piracy. Using Native labor, the Spanish dug out the wealth, specifically gold and silver, in South America and sent it back to Spain.

By the mid-1550s, the Spanish New World became a target for attacks on Spanish shipping and coastal cities. These acts of piracy were first committed by the French, and later the Dutch and English joined in on the raids. Corsairs and privateers were essentially pirates who plundered ships with government approval and agreed to give a portion of their treasure to the crown. National rivalries, greed, and religious differences fueled the attacks on the Spanish Main, which by the late 1500s included Spanish holdings on the mainland in South America and the islands in the Caribbean and the coastline in the Gulf of Mexico. By the early 1600s, the French, Dutch, and English secured a number of toeholds among the islands of the West Indies.

Although there is a proliferation of peg legs in late 19th century fiction and 20th century film, the reality says otherwise, and in fact only two pirates have been referred to by their wooden walking aid, according to author Jan Rogozinski. François Le Clerc was a 16th century French Corsair. Based in Normandy, Le Clerc financed voyages and commanded his own ships. As one of the first to board opposing ships, he lost his leg and damaged his arm, possibly against the British in 1549. In 1551, he was elevated to nobility for his bravery in battle. Le Clerc led seven pirate ships and three royal warships against Spain in raids on Puerto Rico and Hispaniola in 1553. He returned a year later with eight ships that decimated the town of Santiago on the island of Cuba. Following the power and the money, Le Clerc switched sides in 1563 and terrorized French shipping on behalf of the English and died that same year.

Cornelius Corneliszoon Jol lost his leg at a young age, but was said to be just as able as his crewmembers. A Dutch pirate, Jol was active in the Caribbean from 1626 until his death in 1641. He led 10 major raids with ships, crew, and supplies from the Dutch West India Company, a private company authorized to trade in the West Indies. Although fellow Dutch Pirate Piet Heyn took more treasure, Jol's attacks were so frequent and deadly, the Spanish, his primary target, nicknamed him el pirata, but he could also have been nicknamed "Houtebeen," Dutch for peg leg. "He was the pirate above all others and mere rumors of his arrival created panic... With little education and fewer words, most of them unprintable, Jol's quick temper, roughness, and lack of tact were as legendary as his courage."

Despite his brutality, Jol, unlike other pirates and perhaps because he did not want to deal with live cargo, was embarrassed by slavery and on at least two occasions he set Spanish slave ships free.

From 1626-1635, Jol owned and captained the *Otter*, a Dutch yacht. He joined forces off the Brazilian coast with other Dutch pirates including Dierk van Uytgeest. By 1630 he had joined forces with other pirates under the Dutch West India Company and led raids over Brazil. Under Jol's command they took three ships and destroyed a fleet of 30 or more Spanish ships. It's very likely that Jol knew and conducted business with fellow Dutch West Indies employee and future amputee and Director General of New Amsterdam, Peter Stuyvesant, who you will hear more about in a later chapter.

Jol stepped up his adventures and deceptions in 1636 after being ordered to Curaçao, which the Dutch captured in 1634, to protect the arrival of a Dutch fleet. Bored with guard duty, he decided to invade Santiago de Cuba. Jol's ships flew the Spanish flag and his crew wore monks' robes. They entered the harbor under the Spanish gunfire and raided several ships, most of which were empty. In 1636 he headed back for Curaçao commanding a war ship and two yachts, and for six months he sailed between the Gulf of Mexico and an island off southwestern Haiti. Other attacks and raids were carried out with varying degrees of success and failure. Jol died in 1641 from West African diseases, which he was exposed to when he captured a Portuguese slave depot at Luanda and Sâo Thomé. After a festive burial, the Portuguese retook the town a year later, dug up Jol's grave, and scattered his bones.

Oñate and New Mexico

K. "In 1998, on the four hundredth anniversary of Oñate's expedition to New Mexico, the (statue's) foot disappeared. 'Someone came in the middle of the night and cut it off,' Max said. 'Sliced clean through the bronze. Must have used a power grinder.' ...The statue's sculptor had since attached a new foot, and the repair was barely visible. But the original foot had never been found."

One of the five richest men in New Spain, Don Juan de Oñate offered his "services for the discovery, pacification, and conversion of the said provinces of New Mexico" to King Phillip II in 1595. Oñate was the son of Cristobal de Oñate, the discoverer of the Zacatecas mines, and he proposed to pay for the discovery and settlement "all at my cost." The king responded favorably, appointing him Governor, captain, and general, granting him full power. The colony was funded and operated by a private licensed entrepreneur or adelantado, commonly called a proprietor in England. After considering the Native population, the King added, "You will. . .attract the natives with peace, friendship, and good treatment, with which I particularly charge you, and to induce them to hear and accept the holy gospel." The expedition, with 130 families and approximately 400 people, 83 wagons, and 7,000 head of livestock, stretched along the trail for four miles. On January 26, 1598, they departed Santa Barbara, the northernmost town in Mexico.

When Oñate took possession of the kingdom for Phillip II on April 30, a royal notary took down every word. "I take and seize tenancy and possession of lands, pueblos, cities, towns, castles, fortified and unfortified houses, which are now established in the kingdoms and said provinces of New Mexico." Oñate then took a cross, nailed it to a tree and dropped to his knees and offered a prayer to spread the glory of God to the Natives, and asked to "open to us a way of peace and safety for their conversion."

At the confluence of the Rio Grande and Rio Chama, some 20 miles north of modern day Santa Fe and 800 miles from where his journey started, Oñate settled colonists in a Native town and established a capital. On August 11, 1598, he named the capital of New Mexico, San Juan De Los Caballeros, or St. John of the Knights. Eleven days later, as required by the crown, "the building of the church was started and it was completed on September 7." They did not, as the law required, build houses for their settlers. They took over the Native American Tewa-speaking pueblos. A celebration was held in which all the tribes attended. Soldiers fired muskets and harquebuses to display Spanish power and a play was performed; the entertainment closed with a bullfight.

Oñate then set out on another exploration, but this time he headed west. His nephew, Juan de Zaldivar, set out to meet their party with thirty soldiers. Zaldivar reached the Acoma nation, which was built on a flat crown of mesa nearly 400 feet high. Zaldivar was seeking food and blankets for his men. Once the soldiers reached the top, the order to attack was given by Chief Zutucupan. Zaldivar and ten other soldiers were killed. Returning from his expedition, Oñate heard of the killing of his nephew; after consulting with the Franciscan Friars, who gave their approval, Oñate's order sought to "make war by blood and fire" against the pueblo of the Acoma. This war was to be carried out by his other nephew and Juan's brother, Vincente de Zaldivar, and seventy soldiers. After three days and the slaughter of more than 200 Native Americans, the Acoma elders surrendered, and Vincente took the rest, 80 men and 500 women and children, to St. John.

In February 1599, Oñate, acting as judge and jury, listened only to the testimony of the Spanish soldiers. Children were taken from parents and put in the care of Franciscan priests. Acoma over 12 years of age were condemned to personal servitude of colonists. On February 12, Oñate sentenced all Acoma men over the age of 25 to have one foot cut off and give 20 years of service, similar to an indentured servant, as slavery was prohibited. The order was to be carried out in public at pueblos near Santa Fe to send a message to other Natives. The sentence was not, as historian John Kessell suggests, commuted at the last minute to show their superiority and generosity, because evidence verifying this act does not exist. Past horrors perpetrated by Conquistadors, as well as English Colonial leaders, prove the rule of cruelty rather than exceptions. In fact, a year later, Governor Oñate hanged two Native chiefs, killed six Indians, and burned a town, he said, "in a tactful and gentle way" after soldiers were insulted. The uneasy peace that resulted after the sentencing also indicates that the legs were cut off and instilled fear in the Pueblo peoples, whose population of 60,000 heavily outnumbered the 400 Spanish colonists. All the Natives likely died as a result of the severing, from the shock, blood loss, or the lethal combination.

Captain Luis Gasco de Velasco wrote to the viceroy in Mexico that the first acts of abuse had come from the soldiers and that the Acoma had defended themselves and referred to Oñate's punishments as "pitiful" and "cruel." Velasco also heard Vincente de Zaldivar address Oñate as "Your Majesty." In 1609, Oñate resigned before the official recall reached him and he left New Mexico. Five years later he was facing criminal charges for his actions. He was acquitted of murders and for the "assumption of royal airs," but he was convicted of inhumane severity in the war on the Acoma and the punishment of the Indians who survived.

He returned to Spain to plead his case. In 1624, at the age of 75, Oñate was pardoned by King Phillip III and the title of adelantado was bestowed for life.

The MVP of Amputees

I sat in the chair at Sport Clips in Fairhope, Alabama, and ordered my haircut. "Can I take your glasses?" I handed them to the raven-haired round-faced stylist and she put them on the counter in front of the mirror. We made the usual small talk.

"Who cuts your hair?" and "Have you been to Sport Clips before?" I liked all the questions. It reminded me of my reporting days when I would ask the questions, but often it turned conversational. We had good banter.

"What kind of gel do you use?"

"I don't know; I just borrow my wife's."

"You should get the MVP, it's like a mini spa," she said, and she wasn't smiling, but I could tell I was being sold to.

"Plus, it's actually a dollar cheaper than the regular haircut. It's eleven dollars." Now I was interested and decided to MVP.

"Your hair is so thick," she said, complimentarily.

"In some places," I said, about the top, an area I call the cone of uncertainty.

"No, you're fine," she said, and oddly that reassured me coming from her. I think she was being honest.

"This side's wanting to stick up already; you sure you want the top a little shorter?"

"No. Better leave it."

After the cut, she blew off the hair, and took off the apron around my neck.

"Did you tear your ACL?"

She gestured toward my knee, noticing the seam, which looks like a brace.

"No," I told her lifting my pant leg, "I wear a prosthesis."

"Oh," she said casually, then added "my uncle's a triple amputee and my granddad's an amputee too."

71

"He jokes about it a lot," she said about her uncle, something to the effect that he was a risk taker who lived about a two-hour drive away.

"He's Country," I said. She giggled, nodded, smiled.

"Oh, yeah."

We moved to the sink, and continued the conversation about her uncle as she was washing my hair.

She put the hot towel around my face, not over my nose and mouth, and asked if I was comfortable.

"I'll probably keep talking, even with the towel over my mouth." It was very relaxing.

"My uncle was electrocuted."

I had the towel over my face, she was washing my hair, careful not to spray water in my ear, and I really was enjoying the beginning of my mini spa, until she jolted me awake.

"He was electrocuted?"

"Yeah. He was working in a bucket, you know, on a truck, and got electrocuted. It was about 16 years ago, so I was little."

"They couldn't save his legs. My granddad lost his in the war, he's an above knee but my uncle's are both below knee."

"Mine was a birth defect but they amputated more when I was a kid. I didn't experience the trauma that your family did, especially your uncle."

"There are so many different stories though, and you were a kid, so I'm sure that was tough."

"Do you have problems or pain? I've heard them talking about it sometimes," she said.

"Yeah, sometimes, but this leg's been pretty good so far."

"They complain about how it fits."

"If the leg is wrong from the start, no matter what they do it seems like it's never right and you're better off to just start from scratch."

We moved back to the chair for the neck and shoulder massage with one of those handheld massagers.

"I broke my toe once when I kicked my uncle's leg," she said and I saw myself laughing in the mirror. "He wasn't wearing them when I did it."

"Well, I left my leg on the floor once and my wife kicked it and broke her toe." She was facing away from the mirrors, but I heard her laughing.

"That's just who they are," she said of her family. Yeah, that's what my family says about me. They never treated me any differently because they have known me no other way.

"Okay, how's it look?"

I looked, then asked, "Could you hand me my glasses?"

She did.

"It looks good," I said, after viewing it from multiple mirror angles.

As we walked to the register, I said, "Do you have a card?"

She grabbed a generic one from the holder near the cash register as I grabbed one from my wallet and wrote my blog name on the back.

"I've got a sense of humor, but not as good as your uncle."

She wrote her name on the back. Nikki, in stick-like letters that looked like the hash mark lines I use to count reference and computer questions at the library.

When I got into the car to look at the cut, the spot Nikki told me was going to stand up, stuck out like a sore stump, just like our amputee stories.

ALAN L. SAMRY

4. Biography

L. "Perhaps there is no history, only biography."

Out on a Limb on St. Charles Street in
New Orleans on Halloween

Beauty Scars

Part I

Standing beside the black table
her nude form, back, buttocks, and legs
reflect in the mirror.
The image is cut in half by the black iron trim that sections
the mirror.
Her body floats above me as if submerged in water
skin glistening in my imagined wetness
There is weightlessness in her image
and she is bigger than herself, somehow.
She teases and tantalizes on bended ankle
Her skin, so cool smooth to the touch, I wanted it for my
own.

Her outstretched Achilles whispers to me.
The pain in my clouded heart stops
at the moment of her deliberate mercy.
I shined in the sun, a moment
of sweetness within a darkened star,
until she feels my hand with her forehead.
Touching the stubble on her shin makes me shiver.
I forget who I am and spill my
fingertips over her thigh and a jaunty dusting
of pleasure captures all my senses
destroying my anger and closing the distance
between our still, silent, forms.

Part II

The tiny scar on the back
of her thigh glows white
I resist touching it.
I want to touch it.
To feel the fault line between
slicing pain and healed flesh
It seems a dream
this slice of hers
A sandscaped crest of a
P-Town dune above
Damp gray fog, slowly
lifting, or burning off.
The breach of the white whale
 in a sea of blue

Stump skin is purple
cold in the morning.
Emerges white
hot upon evening socket escape.
Unshapely,
desolate, hairless, jagged scar tissue
Bony
protuberances, or ugly
undulations
 bound by asymmetrical stitches.
A slab of fatback
bulges behind my knee.
Distal end is a toothless
blacken-blued Great White.
The crisscross stitches
jump the hole left behind

After my so-called
toes were "osteotomized."

Part III

At the sight of an un-whole man with a hole, she recoils
her scar
Quickly gathers scattered clothes and scurries out
the door.
I float in an unfulfilled sea yearning for her intimate flaw
Swimming in a drowning desire to know the infinite
beauty of loss.

Earl Fogler

"I was in second grade here in Houston," Earl Fogler told *O and P Edge* magazine, as he recalled the schoolyard bombing at Edgar Allan Poe Elementary in 1959. On September 15, seven-year-old Fogler was injured in the bombing, losing part of his right leg just below the knee. The explosion killed six people, including the bomber and his son, and injured 18 others.

"We were at our morning recess," Fogler said, recalling a man and his son coming onto the playground with a suitcase.

"At some point during his conversation with the principal and some other teachers, he set the suitcase down and dynamite went off," Fogler remembered, marking one of the earliest acts of schoolyard violence in United States history. He remained hospitalized for several weeks at Hermann Hospital, where he was operated on by a Korean War field surgeon veteran.

He returned to school in mid-October and his family documented the event. "I have a picture of my first day, using crutches," he said. In the photograph, his crutches help support the weight of his missing leg. His jeans are cuffed up on both legs practically up to his kneecap. Perhaps a way for his mom to balance out the fact that one of the pant legs is empty. Aside from that, he is a smiling boy with a crew cut, wearing a jacket with a book bag clinging to him from a shoulder strap and he's grabbing his lunch box and crutch handle with his right hand.

Henry Highland Garnet

Henry Highland Garnet was born in Maryland into an enslaved family in 1815. When he was 10 his father George, upon the death of their owner, secured passes for his family and escaped from Maryland to Wilmington, Delaware, ultimately reaching New York City in 1825. When he was a child, Henry suffered from a "sports injury." George Garnet became a Presbyterian minister after the slave revolts, and joined the antislavery movement of antebellum America. Henry was a well-known part of the community as he often attended conferences and all facets of early black community meetings with his father, George Garnet. Through Henry's education and ministry, he became an impressive, persuasive, and radical orator among black abolitionists.

The front page of the December 12, 1840 edition of the *The Colored American*, an African American newspaper that Garnet wrote for, reports:

> "Our esteemed friend and brother, Garnet has had to submit to the painful process of having the limb with which he has so long been aflicted, amputated, and from which process he is now suffering great indisposition. His friend...will his case to the Father of mercies and spared long to live to be a blessing to our oppressed people.
>
> P.S. News has just been received that brother Garnet is quite comfortable."

By 1841, Garnet was a prominent figure in the Northern abolitionist community, and was a member of the Liberty Party, America's first antislavery political party. Garnet was a tall, fiery minister who preached from the pulpit or at antislavery meetings about slave resistance as a measure to change the status quo of enslavement in the South. Garnet's dark skin reflected his African heritage and his deep brown eyes commanded attention, while his square forehead contrasted with his mutton chop beard. The black convention movement occurred between 1830 and 1864 at the national, state, and local level where black leaders like Garnet, Frederick Douglass, and Martin Delany spoke.

Garnet was involved in several different antislavery social movement organizations, including the New York African Free School, the Liberty Party, and the American Colonization Society and generally the black convention movement. In the quest to abolish slavery, the black community organized all of its social movements within the church. It is evident that Garnet was the leader in this community. In 1841, Garnet ministered an all-black congregation at Troy, New York's Liberty Street Presbyterian Church. The church hosted the New York Negro Convention that same year. In addition, Garnet recognized the importance of education and he established a school for black children, which was housed in the church basement. To get a turnout for these conventions, pamphlets were used to distribute information and it was likely advertised and written about in the abolition newspapers. Garnet was a firm believer in the black press and expressed his own views in his newspaper, *The Clarion*. He also published the *National Watchman* from 1842 to 1847. In addition, his views were expressed elsewhere in the media as Garnet and other prominent blacks wrote articles for *The Liberator* and *The North Star*.

Henry Highland Garnet. National Portrait Gallery, Smithsonian Institution, 1892, by James U. Stead

Race, Equality, and Disability

Disabilities Studies scholar Douglas Baynton questions the role disability plays in America's history. He refers to disability as the "next academic frontier," but it remains to be seen whether disability will rank among the holy trinity of academic significance: race, class, and gender. However, when we look at Garnet's battle for rights, we can see directly how citizenship and disability have been marginalized in America's past. In this vein, Garnet had two strikes against ever attaining full citizenship: his color and his status as a cripple.

It's important to consider how blacks, and more specifically crippled blacks, were viewed at the time when looking at Garnet's speech. In his speech, "Let Your Motto Be Resistance," Garnet is always trying to identify with the slaves and even calls them "Fellow Citizens." His speech, given with fifty-eight black abolitionist delegates in attendance, provides a history of slavery in America and places the blame on the colonial Christians and Founding Fathers. Of Blacks taken from Africa to America, Garnet explains, "Neither did they come flying upon wings of Liberty, to a land of freedom." He also makes a stern moral argument for freeing the enslaved.

Garnet calls Jefferson's Declaration of Independence a "glorious document," but of the founders he asks and then answers with contempt, "Were they ignorant of the principles of liberty? Certainly they were not." He continued to apply the Revolutionary War rhetoric like "LIBERTY OR DEATH."

Baynton is helpful in placing Garnet into historical perspective as disability is used to justify inequality in citizenship debates for African American freedom. In the early 19th century, many doctors believed that African Americans, due to their physical and mental weakness, "were prone to become disabled under conditions of freedom and equality." Doctors believed at the time that "if freedom for African Americans was undesirable and slavery good, then it was sufficient to note that free blacks were more likely than slaves to be disabled." Despite his pleadings, how could Garnet speak for slaves when he could not attain freedom for himself? "Fundamental nature of physical experience, the life-altering power of an acquired disability, the human tendency to classify and rank others on the basis of appearance," Baynton believes, is what makes disability significant. It is this type of backward thinking that supported white superiority and fed into feelings of black inferiority that Garnet tried to free himself and his audience from. Garnet rose to a position of leadership through education and theology, but he also recognized the difficulties and barriers to citizenship while being black and crippled.

Garnet visualized a nonviolent slave resistance that would fuel a new African American identity. His goal was to strike a balance between the suffering servant and the violent radicals, where both could find a common goal to stand up to their oppressors and demand freedom and basic human rights.

Garnet simply could not identify with the group of violent radicals, or those patiently waiting for slave owners to be persuaded to change from their immoral practices. Garnet formulated this middle ground of nonviolent resistance, at least in part, because of his disability. Garnet's experience, character, and physical image after the amputation leads Garnet to middle ground. Garnet's wooden leg no longer allowed him to participate in violent resistance and this would have had an effect on his speech. If he could no longer run, he could not advocate running away (though he did provide shelter and food for runaway slaves on the Underground Railroad). Consciously or subconsciously, Garnet took into account his physical limitation and compromised.

Garnet's Experience

In 1848, five years after his most famous speech, Garnet tells of an experience he had while he was a passenger on a train. Garnet was told he could not sit with Southern white men and women. Garnet explained his reaction to an audience:

> "This was not a sufficient reason to [move] my seat and not being accustomed to yielding my rights without making at least a semblance of lawful resistance, I quietly returned towards my seat. I was prevented by the conductor, who seized me violently by the throat, and choked me severely." (Winkelman 17)

What an appropriate example of nonviolent resistance where the blood is on the hands of the oppressors, just like Garnet communicates in his speech. The event strikes familiar notes from America's more recent nonviolent resistance attempts. On a Montgomery, Alabama, bus, Rosa Parks refused to give up her seat on December 1, 1955 and violated a local segregation ordinance. The Freedom Rides of 1961 tested the interstate transportation desegregation ruling and proved Garnet correct again when the bus was firebombed, and the riders brutally beaten by a mob of segregationists in Anniston, Alabama. However, as Garnet continues to tell the audience about his own experience, it becomes obvious that it's more than just racial:

> "I have for many years been a cripple. I made no resistance further than was necessary to save myself from injury assaulted; but nonetheless, this conductor and another person, whose name I do not know continued to choke and to assault me with the first. A part of the time my legs were under the cars near the wheels, and several persons were crying out – 'don't kill him, don't kill him!'" (Winkelman 18)

This event in Garnet's own words speaks volumes about how the rhetoric of protest cannot be separated from Garnet's experiences in dealing with citizenship, race, and disability. By not putting Garnet into historical perspective with regard to his disability, we are in fact simplifying his experiences.

To gain a better understanding of Garnet or any complex person from our past is difficult. It's important to remember that Garnet was a black person who beat the odds. He escaped from slavery, had a leg amputated, and became the second most prominent black abolitionist during the mid-1800s. He was a spiritual, political, educational, and community leader, and he accomplished it all while standing on a wooden leg.

Virginia Hall

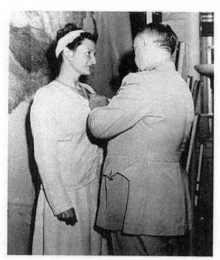

Virginia Hall receiving the Distinguished Service Award from General
Donovan (Central Intelligence Agency Website)

Anyone who gives their prosthesis a nickname has to be in my book. But Virginia Hall is no ordinary amputee or woman. She was America's greatest female spy and a leader in the French Resistance that helped fight the Nazis during World War II. Hall was known as The Limping Lady, was a master of disguise, and operated under several aliases, according to the definitive biography, *The Wolves at the Door*, by Judith Pearson.

"The woman who limps is one of the most dangerous Allied agents in France. We must find and destroy her," is what one Gestapo flyer said about Hall.

In the winter of 1933, when she was twenty-seven years old, an accident altered Hall's career goal of working with the State Department.

While employed at the US Embassy in Turkey, she went on a hunting trip with friends and coworkers. She accidentally shot her left foot. So far from a hospital, the wound quickly became gangrenous. The leg was amputated just below the knee. After recuperating from the surgery, she returned to the US to have a wooden leg made. After she made several failed attempts to get promoted in the State Department, Assistant Secretary of State Sumner Welles wrote, "Amputation of any portion of a limb is...cause for rejection." Without being able to move up the State Department ladder, she resigned.

She stayed overseas and began aiding in the French Resistance to Nazi occupation. Eventually, Britain's Special Operation Executive, SOE, hired Hall for her existing ties to the resistance and her fluency in French and German. She was sent to Vichy in August 1941 under the name Marie Monin to set up resistance networks, report troop movement, carry messages, and retrieve dropped messages, all while disguised as an elderly milkmaid.

After thirteen months, she was told to return to England for a much-needed break.

Her return included a thirty-mile trek over the Pyrenees in the winter. She sent a radio report to London. "Cuthbert is giving me trouble, but I can cope." Unaware of her leg's nickname, they messaged back, "If Cuthbert is giving you difficulty," they replied, "have him eliminated."

For her spy services, she was awarded the Most Excellent Order of the British Empire, or MBE.

Shortly after, she joined the OSS Office of Strategic Services, America's espionage organization, and learned to become a radio operator.

She was sent back to France, this time as Marcelle Montagne, a slightly hunched older woman who sold goat cheese. Hall altered her gait to hide her limp or rode an old bicycle. During her second tour, her team destroyed four bridges, derailed several freight trains, blew up a railway line, cut telephone wires, and captured hundreds of enemy soldiers.

Hall was awarded the Distinguished Service Cross award, the only American woman and the first civilian to be awarded the honor during WW II. It was in a private service, as she continued to work for the OSS, which later became the Central Intelligence Agency.

In posthumously presenting the MBE certificate in 2006, French President Jacques Chirac said, "Virginia Hall is the true hero of the French Resistance. Her indomitable bravery, her exceptional selflessness, her staunch determination, and her talents as a leader and organizer contributed greatly to the Liberation of France."

James Hanger

I was on lunch break sitting in the glass block-enclosed break room and kitchen of the library. Light streamed in from the near-100-degree day outside. I opened up the latest *Smithsonian* magazine that I'd grabbed from the periodical room on my way to lunch. The magazine chose to remember the 150th anniversary of the Civil War with a page of monthly details. This time it was Philippi, Virginia.

"What's the name on your T-shirt?" my father-in-law John Cherkofsky asked me later that day, when Sue and I were over for hamburgers on the grill. All these years I thought her family said "hamburgers" as a colloquialism that included cheeseburgers. Not so. The family had been cooking cheese-less burgers before my arrival. Sue has only been eating cheeseburgers for twenty years, about as long as we've been married.

"Hanger Prosthetics," I said. "It's a nationwide company that's been making artificial legs since 1861." Pointing down at my leg, I said, "The office in Fairhope made this leg."

Philippi was the first organized land action during the Civil War, just a few months after Confederates pounded Fort Sumter. On June 3rd, a two-pronged attack by Union forces was taken against the Confederates. Taken by surprise in the early morning attack, which was the intent of the Union Army led by General George McClelland, the Rebels retreated, according to newspaper accounts, in their pajamas. It became known as the "Races at Philippi."

An 18-year-old engineering student at Washington College (Washington and Lee College today), James Edward Hanger joined the Confederate Army. Less than two days after enlisting on June 1, 1861, while standing guard outside a barn, Hanger heard cannon fire and went inside. A cannon ball came through the wall and struck Hanger in the leg. Dr. James D. Robinson, a Union surgeon, performed the battlefield amputation and removed his leg mid-thigh, thereby making Hanger the first land-related injury and first amputee of the Civil War.

> "I cannot look back upon those days in the hospital without a shudder. No one can know what such a loss means unless he has suffered similar catastrophe. In the twinkling of an eye, life's fondest hopes seemed dead. I was the prey of despair. What could the world hold for a maimed crippled man!"

While a prisoner of war, Hanger was fitted with a peg, and was released in August 1861.

In November 1861, Hanger descended the stairs from his upstairs bedroom wearing the prosthesis he designed and built by whittling barrel staves. Of the "Hanger Limb" its maker stated, "Today I am thankful for what seemed then to me nothing but a blunder of fate, but which was to prove instead a great opportunity."

Peg Leg Lonergan

If I hadn't watched Season Three of *Boardwalk Empire*, starring Steve Buscemi, I never would have discovered him. *Boardwalk Empire* is a fantastic HBO series, loosely based on the life of Atlantic City politician and crime boss, Enoch "Nucky" Johnson, set during Prohibition. In the episode, Nucky calls a meeting of all the New York gangsters together and mentions a guy by the name of "Peg Leg Lonergan." It turns out James "Peg Leg" Lonergan is based on a real person.

Lonergan, born in Brooklyn, New York, in 1900, lost his right leg in a trolley car accident when he was 10, earning his now infamous moniker. A few years later, a family member gave him a bicycle, which he couldn't ride with or without a prosthesis. Instead of selling the bike, he decided to rent it out. The business model became so popular that he bought more bikes to rent out, according to *Paddy Whacked: The Untold Story of the Irish American Gangster*, by T. J. English. Eventually, he bought a shop where he bought, sold, and rented bikes.

An Italian by the name of Bonanzio asked Lonergan if he could sell drugs in front of his store, R.J.L Sporting Goods. Peg Leg replied, not with a simple no—he beat the crap out of Bonanzio, who later sought revenge and had someone sell Lonergan a stolen bike. The Italian ratted him out to the police, and Lonergan was sent away to a work farm. That's where he met Wild Bill Lovett, a future gang leader and brother-in-law.

Credited by his sister for killing 20 men, Peg Leg eventually headed up the White Hand Gang, the Irish Mob, not to be confused with the Black Hand, which was not a gang, but a description of methods Italians used for their criminal deeds.

Lonergan, after an illustrious career as a racketeer, bootlegger, hit man, and crime boss, met his end on Christmas

Day, 1925, according to *Paddy Whacked*. After a night of hard drinking, Lonergan and three cronies walked into the Adonis Social Club, an Italian speakeasy. One Irishman was called over to a table of Italian gangsters, including one Al Capone. After a bottle was smashed over the head of an Irishman, a fracas broke out and a shootout ensued. When it was over, three of the four Irish mobsters were dead, including Lonergan. Capone was questioned, but never charged, according to *Paddy Whacked*. Subsequent evidence determined that Capone was one of the shooters.

Gouverneur Morris:
America's Disabled Founding Father

"We, the People of the United States, in Order to form a more perfect Union, to establish Justice, insure domestic Tranquility, provide for the common defense, promote the general Welfare, and secure the Blessings of Liberty to ourselves and our Posterity, do ordain and establish this Constitution for the United States of America."

George Washington, John Adams, Thomas Jefferson, Alexander Hamilton, James Madison, and Benjamin Franklin are names Americans all know. They are celebrated as major figures during the founding of America between 1776 with the Declaration of Independence, the American Revolution, the ratification of the Constitution in 1788, and the decision by President George Washington in 1797 to refuse a third term. These men provided sound leadership during the Constitutional Convention in Philadelphia when the direction of the nation was uncertain.

One man was charged with writing the final version of the constitution. His name, little known today outside Constitutional historians and scholars, was Gouverneur Morris. Morris, a New York aristocrat, was in the company of America's founding fathers, and was called upon by them to finalize the underpinnings of a new national government. Morris was a man of physical stature, being as tall as George Washington. An early portrait shows a man with distinguishing features including a forehead full of hair that extended below his neck and tied at the end in a bow. His subtle jaw line and brown eyes were contrasted by his full lips, eagle-beaked nose and furrowed brow. Since the Morrises were part of New York's elite families for 100 years, he also had tremendous social stature. As a signer of the Articles of Confederation and the New York Constitution, Morris also had a strong political reputation.

The assignment was bestowed upon Morris by a committee of men who knew about his boisterous and sometimes overbearing personality, yet they trusted him enough; and he was the one capable of setting aside his personal views to ensure the decisions of the convention were written succinctly. Morris's writing had to outline the complex details of the resolutions of the Constitutional Convention of 1787 in plain language. The man who single handedly wrote the Preamble, Gouverneur Morris, also edited, revised, and rewrote the document we know today as the United States Constitution. Morris accomplished all this standing on a peg leg, after losing his left leg in a carriage accident in 1780.

New York Beginnings

In 1774, Morris, like the majority of Americans, was not looking for independence from England. As a member of the New York Provincial Congress, Morris advocated and helped to establish a new government for New York. He introduced an article, which later failed, that would have prohibited domestic slavery. Although he initially thought reconciliation with England was possible, he understood what was at stake when America began ringing the bell for independence. He also understood the consequences of such actions, saying, "Great revolutions of empire are seldom achieved without much human calamity." In one letter to his mother, Morris refers to himself as a "rebel," as many who supported independence from Britain were branded. In 1777, while New York was occupied with British troops, Morris and other delegates ratified the New York State Constitution. Between 1778 and 1779 Morris served on the Continental Congress and signed the Articles of Confederation. He moved to Philadelphia in 1779. It was the largest city in the colonies at the time and bustled with activity at schools, libraries, newspapers, and two hospitals. For recreation, Morris joined the Schuylkill Fishing Company. As a member of the Schuylkill, founded in 1732 and considered the oldest angling club in America, Morris enjoyed fishing and swimming in the river. He also played quoits, which was similar to horseshoes, where a quoit, or flattened ring of iron, was thrown at a pin. In 1780, while Morris prepared for the Pennsylvania Bar, an accident occurred that left any future recreation in doubt.

Crippling Carriage Crash

How Morris came to lose his leg is still up for debate. Some offer that in mounting his lightweight four-wheeled carriage, or phaeton, pulled by two horses, he was thrown. Others speculate that he was thrown while driving through the streets. The result was that his left leg was caught in the spoke of the wheel in an accident on Dock Street in Philadelphia. The most accurate account is a letter written by William Churchill Houston to Philip Schuyler on the day following the accident and was included in Melanie Miller's book, *An Incautious Man*. Houston, in the letter dated May 15, 1780, writes:

"I am unhappy this Morning to inform you of an accident which happened yesterday to Mr. Gouverneur Morris. He was riding out in a phaeton, and the horses taking a fright ran away in the street, struck the carriage against a post, broke it all to pieces and the shock fractured Mr. Morris's Ancle (sic) to such a degree that it became necessary to take off his leg immediately. He bore the operation with amazing firmness. I have not seen him but am told this morning, that though his fever is pretty high and he has a good deal of pain he is not in danger of life. The bruises he received in the fall are a great addition to the principal accident. There was no person with him in the carriage." (44)

With his regular physician Dr. John Jones away, several doctors were summoned. Morris, in excruciating pain, retained his wits about him and explained that whoever performed the procedure would become famous. After the doctors recommended amputation, Morris responded:

"Gentlemen, I see around me the eminent men of your profession, all acknowledged competent to the performance of the operation. You have already secured renown, the capital by which you live. Now the removal of my leg cannot add to your celebrity; is there not one among you younger in your calling who might perform the act, and secure éclat or his benefit?" (Kirschke 116-117)

Although he did not gain éclat, or great acclaim and notoriety for his operation, Dr. James Hutchinson performed the high below-the-knee amputation. Hutchinson was young, but he was a Continental Army surgeon, and served as Pennsylvania's surgeon general throughout the Revolutionary War. Few physicians in America performed more surgeries than Hutchinson, whose amputation was done well. A tribute to his skill is that Morris never required any stump revisions, or additional surgeries to remove flesh or bone. Jones would later question the need for the amputation. Jones, who founded New York Hospital and wrote the first American textbook on surgery in 1775, may have been correct, but he never actually saw the injury.

Leg History and Leg-ends

Author Richard Brookhiser states that Morris would "later experiment with false legs of copper and cork." This statement requires clarification and explanation. Today as then two types of legs were developed. An exoskeletal prosthesis has a post, main shaft, or shank for support but is encased with fiberglass, carbon fiber, or soft foam. An endoskeletal prosthesis simply means there is no cover to hide the post, which is more common among amputees today, especially men. The copper Brookhiser refers to is the exoskeletal material used to cover the wooden core. An early example of this leg dates back to 1696, when it was developed by Dutch physician Pieter Verduyn. The leg had a wooden foot and post with a copper shell.

Confusion arises over the history of cork legs. A. A. Marks, one of two prominent prosthetic leg manufacturers in the United States in the mid-1800s, explained that the cork leg was a sobriquet or misnomer for an artificial leg in general. Further, he adds that cork was never used in artificial legs because cork is pliable and not strong enough to form part of the support structure. The exact origin of the term is lost, but several theories dating back to the early 1800s should be noted. Londoner James Potts designed a leg in 1800 with a wood shank and socket, a steel knee joint, and a hinged foot controlled by catgut tendons from the knee to the ankle. The leg became associated with its prominent wearer Henry William, Lord Paget, the first Marquess of Anglesey of Oxford, England. The leg has been referred to, most notably, as the "Anglesey Leg," but also as the "Clapper Leg" for its distinct wooden foot clapping sound. Lastly, it has been referred to as the "Cork Leg" for two possible reasons: the legs were made by James Potts on Cork Street in London, or the legs were shipped from County Cork, Ireland, which was an area that became known later for making their own limbs. Legs were simply referred to by amputees by their place of manufacture, and were called "New York Leg" or "London Leg" or "Cork Leg." Since Morris traveled extensively in Europe from 1788-1798, he most likely tested the latest in prosthetic innovations in England and France, and it's possible that he even donned an early version of Potts's "Cork Leg." The Anglesey Leg, as described above, did not arrive in America until 1840.

With the weight of the copper plating, Morris put his trust in oak, a leg he continued to wear throughout his life. The thirty-six-inch-long peg leg had a leather cover for the end of his stump to rest on between a pair of securing wooden arms. The leg appears to be made from one solid piece of oak. Morris biographer James Kirschke does a fine history on the amputation, but fails to mention how the prosthesis stays on. The socket and wood post on the Richard Brookhiser book cover show straps around the thigh and wooden arms are possible to prevent "pistoning" or having the residual limb, or stump, move up and down with every step inside the leg, but they would have likely been secured under his trousers. In a photograph of the actual leg there appears to be some hardware at the end of the wooden arm on the outside of his hip. This suggests that a pelvic strap was used for suspension to hold the leg on.

Contributions to the Constitution

The Constitutional Convention opened May 25, 1787, and members quickly agreed to elect Washington the president of the convention and to keep the proceedings secret. Ultimately, Morris was influential in the design of the Senate, the creation of a strong executive, and in the interrelated issues of westward expansion and slavery. The issue of slavery was the source of what most scholars believe was one of the greatest orations, recorded by James Madison, of the convention and of Morris's career.

"Upon what principle is it that the slaves shall be computed in the representation? Are they Men? Then make them Citizens & let them vote. Are they property? Why then is no other property included?"

Morris was frustrated by the divisions between the North and South over slavery, which he called "the curse of heaven on the States where it prevailed." Despite Morris's eloquent pleadings, the delegates agreed to count the slaves as three-fifths of a person and to enact the Fugitive Slave Law.

After reworking, revising, and rewriting the articles of the Constitution, Morris wrote the Preamble. Morris began the new Preamble, "We, the people," which provides us, even today, with an unmistakable sense of nationalism and unity. Patrick Henry, who refused to attend the convention, recognized the importance and was impressed by the shift to "the people instead of the states."

On September 17, 1787, thirty-eight delegates signed the document and went to City Tavern to rehash the summer events over dinner and Madeira. The United States Constitution was ratified by New Hampshire, which cast the ninth vote on June 21, 1788.

Regarding the pending constitution, Morris wrote a French gentleman, "I have many reasons to believe that it was the work of plain, honest men, and such I think it will appear. Faulty it must be, for what is perfect." Testimony of his heavy involvement comes from Madison.

> "The finish given to the style and arrangement of the Constitution fairly belongs to the pen of Mr. Morris…. A better choice could not have been made, as the performance of the task proved." (Adams 63)

Further evidence of his role in the Constitution comes directly from Morris himself, who writes Timothy Pickering in 1814, stating, "That instrument was written by the fingers which write this letter."

Morris and Friends Weigh in on Leg Loss

Morris and his peers offer us what no other disabled person up to this point in American history has: an honest written record about his disability. Morris and his peers wrote about all facets of his disability, including the amputation and the pain, both real and phantom. In addition, there is humor and sexual innuendo in references to his peg leg. After the amputation, a friend visited Morris and attempted to cheer him up by being the optimist noting that it could have been worse. Morris supposedly responded, "I am almost tempted to part with the other."

Like many who suffered from severe injury and were nursed back to health in the home, Morris fell in love with his caregiver. Mrs. Elizabeth Plater III doted on her patient for several months and it's clear Morris loved her, but it is not clear if it ever became something more.

Letters flew around the continent and across the Atlantic telling of Morris's accident. Most telling of all the letters is perhaps the letter between two women: Sally Jay, John's wife, receives a letter from Mary Morris, who is Robert's (no relation to Gouverneur Morris) wife. Mary writes she was "shocked at irreparable misfortune-the loss of his leg-...I never knew an individual more sympathized with." John Jay writes Robert Morris, who had written Jay of the accident, that "Gouverneur's leg has been a tax on my Heart. I am almost tempted to wish he had lost something else."

Morris did eventually link his leg to something else. He wrote in his diary, if a French woman would experiment with "a native of the new world who had left one of his legs behind him."

Later on, the story of his accident and his amorousness became linked. Although he met the man in Paris only once, Henry Temple recorded in his diary that "Mr. Morris...an American, a gentlemanlike sensible man," lost his leg "in consequence of jumping from a window in an affair of gallantry." There seems to be some question as to who began these rumors, but a few suspects include Jay, the ladies and gentlemen of French society, and Morris himself.

Upon arriving at formal receptions and functions, Morris wrote, "Domestics know not what to make of me, a thing which frequently happens at my first approach, because the simplicity of my dress and equipage, my wooden leg and tone of republican equality, seem totally misplaced at [a] levee."

Other entries about his disability were grounded more in the reality of walking around on a peg leg. Although stump blisters, sores, and abrasions were likely common, one particularly painful episode prompted Morris to record the time he put his stump sock on inside out.

"I remember to have heard, when young, that this portended good luck, and I remember also that, having gone out one morning early I broke my shin before I got back, and in taking down the stocking to look at it found it was wrong side outward. I bear the mark of that misfortune to this hour, a memento not to believe in such sayings."

Morris offers intimate, insightful, and humorous thoughts and experiences in his diaries. We get a glimpse at the reception into the realization that Morris likely received the same stares amputees feel today.

Lasting Legacies

After Morris returned from France he re-entered politics. As a New York Senator in the Sixth Congress, the first to meet in Washington, DC, he served during the presidential election of 1800, which tested the presidential election process as Burr and Jefferson tied with 73 electoral votes. With no majority, the House members voted. After 36 rounds of voting, Jefferson prevailed, with Morris casting a vote for his friend and fellow Federalist, Aaron Burr.

Although he retired from politics in 1803, he remained active in state affairs and took up the pen again and began writing in earnest. Returning to Morrisania, he began writing letters to friends both in the United States and abroad, and wrote essays for the *Evening Post, Examiner, US Gazette*, and often signed his work simply and succinctly as "an American."

Morris again found himself at the center of national events after one of his closest friends, Alexander Hamilton, was killed in a duel in July 1804 by Morris's other friend and fellow New Yorker, Burr. Morris, at the insistence of Hamilton's family, delivered the funeral oration; even in his grief, Morris manages to eloquently describe the loss of his friend, while also attempting to calm the anger directed at Burr. Morris then assumed Hamilton's seat on the board of trustees of his alma mater, now Columbia College.

Morris's other involvement at the state level included his dedication to developing a waterway to tap into the great landlocked resources of the nation, a passion which began in 1800. Morris served on the Erie Canal Commission and became its president in 1811. Morris and other prominent New Yorkers founded the New York Historical Society in the fall of 1804, and eventually went on to serve as the organization's president. As for national security, Morris devised a system of encoding letters sent overseas while he was working in the finance department in 1781. It was slow to encode or decode, but the code lists were used by Morris and later by the United States diplomatic corps and provided secret communications until 1867.

In addition to being considered a genius, according to Madison, "he added what is too rare, a candid surrender of his opinion when the lights of discussion satisfied him that they had been too hastily formed, and a readiness in making the best of measures in which he had been overruled."

His orations at the convention, his eulogy of Washington, and his delivery of the funeral oration for Hamilton show us how Morris was measured by his peers and their families. He was cynical, witty, and romantic and yet spoke his mind. These polar qualities great men possess attract friends and enemies, equally. Historians offer a few sentences on being in the carriage accident and yet they have never drawn connections to his compassion for the underprivileged, especially slaves, and his hope for humankind, despite witnessing the horrors of the French Terror. What stands out is his ability to embellish, enrich, and eroticize his writings to an art. The writings from Morris and the founding fathers provide us a glimpse into the life of a disabled person before socially constructed stereotypes formed in America.

Morris deserves to be recognized as a Founding Father. Although disabled, he played a critical part in documenting the diversity of America that continues to flourish today. Perhaps Morris can be understood best by his independence, an ideal we continue to celebrate in America. It seems ironic and perhaps contradictory that Morris lived his life beholden to no one and a free spirit of 1776 and yet his legacy, "We, the people," transcended that independence and continues to join us together as Americans. The Preamble and the leg Morris wore have stood the test of time. His leg is part of the New York Historical Society's collection and the words of the Preamble are the same as the day Morris put his inked quill to parchment.

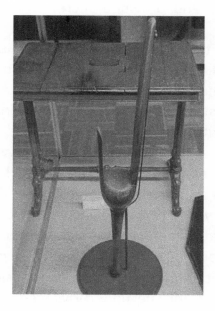

Wooden leg of Gouverneur Morris, New York Historical Society Collection (From Wikipedia Loves Art participant "the_adverse_possessors" https://commons.wikimedia.org/w/index.php?curid=8884194)

The Missing Limb in the Samry Tree

M. "What we call monsters are not so to God."

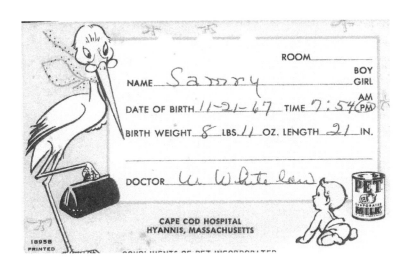

I'm staring at my medical records from Shriners Hospital for Crippled Children. Over the years I've had more unanswered questions about my disability than I can count. I've got scraps of details about my mother's reactions to my birth defect, but until recently I've not known the details of my disability and have begun exploring possible causes or at least clinical diagnoses to explain my limb loss. Here it is some forty years later in smudgy black typewriter ink. Diagnosis: Terminal partial hemimelia, right tibia, fibula. I look up "hemimelia" online: "a congenital abnormality (as total or partial absence) affecting only the distal half of a limb." Is this accurate? Why do I doubt the diagnosis? Do we know more forty years later? What are the complications? Are there complications? A diagnosis merely describes a condition. I have always wanted to know "what happened." I suppose this latest curiosity with my past has something to do with what I'm reading. The essay, "The Creation Myths of Cooperstown," by Stephen Jay Gould rekindled my fascination with my own beginnings. In his essay about the myths and origins of the game of baseball, Gould writes, "We are powerfully drawn to beginnings. We yearn to know about origins." Seeing the records from the past has also made me wonder if there were any myths in the story of my own beginnings.

***

8/3/2010

Hi Ma,

These are copies of my records from Shriners Hospital. I'm hoping you can tell me if that's Dr. Kruger from the hospital in a photo from *Life Magazine*. As I learn more, I'll tell you. In the meantime, review the records. I'm hoping very much to talk to you again about my birth and its consequences. It's part of our story, and I want to tell it. Not just ours, yours and mine, but the Samry/Hannan story. What happened when I was born? I was not a routine birth. Who was there? Was Whitelaw? Where was Dad? I know back then people were not allowed in the delivery room, but was he or anyone at the hospital? Who else can you remember? What did they say after I was delivered? Were you awake, not sure about all the meds and how strong they were? Did the hospital or doctors try to cover their asses legally or in any way? What did the doctors and nurses say once I was born? Did they tell you about the birth defect? Did you see it?

How did people react, including my brothers and sisters, when you told them or they saw me for the first time? Did you hide my leg? That would seem natural at first, I think. It is very meaningful for me to understand what you (and Dad) went through, especially early on. You mentioned the clinic in Hyannis, any more detail about that would be great. You mentioned last week when I was up there visiting that you got sick of answering the same old questions. What were the questions? I'm working on an essay about my early years, the years I can't remember, so I'm relying on you to fill in some of the details as best you can. In my first exam at Shriners there is a doctor mentioned. Maybe he's the clinic doctor.

The question that I've wondered about most was why didn't you baptize me? Faith has been very fleeting for me and that's okay. I've been able to appreciate other spirituality. It must have been tough to keep your own faith when I was born, but I never knew why I was not baptized, given the fact that everyone except Dad was a practicing Catholic up until my birth. What was Dad's take on all this? What did he say? Did you talk about baptizing me? Did someone get in the middle of all this?

I am only trying to join our stories through mutual understanding. What you remember from then and your feelings about it then and now will be hugely helpful. You've read most of my writing so think of this as us being co-writers. Pay particular attention to the details of the first few pages when I was examined. Also when you look at the records make notes. I would love it if you wrote your reactions and memories down. Write on the records if you want. Just write whatever you are thinking on the subject. It sometimes helps. It's called thinking on the page.

Can't wait to see you,

Love,

Alan

***

The Cape Cod Hospital birth announcement card my mom sent me has a white stork clutching a medical bag. Resting on the stork's yellow beak is a pair of pince nez glasses circa FDR. A pink polka dot ribbon flutters around her neck.

In the lower right-hand corner of the three-by-five-inch card is a yellow-haired, white-diapered, pink-skinned baby. Next to the baby and about the same size is a can of PET evaporated milk. The background of the announcement is white, but the border of the card is blue with a few pink ribbons dancing near the edges.

The line below the vitals is blank. A perfect place for something to be written: I imagine cards with stock sayings like "Fuzzy Hair," "Beautiful Baby," or "Ten Fingers and Ten Toes."

The biggest news about my birth didn't make it into print. My disability is unrecorded from the very beginning.

The copy of my birth certificate from the town of Eastham, where we lived when I was born, gives a few more details about my birthday. We lived on Route 6 in Eastham, but oddly no house number is given. Mom was 35 and Dad was 40. My father was a tile setter at the time and my mom took care of her four children at home. Pretty rare these days, but common back in 1967. The certificate lists me as male and white. Both my parents' places of birth are listed as Brockton. In the announcement I was just a Samry, now I'm Alan Lester Samry.

No record of my birth defect exists on paper at the moment or near the moment I entered the world. This bugs me. Didn't anyone care enough to write it down? Doctors are trained to write things down, keep records of their patients. Aren't they required by law to do this?

I have three documents recording my birth, actually four, counting the newspaper clipping from the *Cape Cod Times* newspaper. None of them mention anything about a defect, even though I didn't have a right foot after exiting the birth canal.

***

My mom's one-bedroom apartment is on the second story of a four-story affordable housing building in Falmouth, Massachusetts. She hates the couch I'm sitting on, though she's had it for ten years or more. She usually sits in her pink recliner. The walls are still smoke-stained yellow even though she quit five years ago. Her wavy gray hair needs a trim, she says. Her

78-year-old cheeks are sunken, but her blue eyes, when open, are crisp and alert behind her brown-framed glasses. Her upper dentures sit on a paper plate on her white laminate folding table where she eats most of her meals, pays her bills, and watches TV. A Red Sox game is blaring at conversation-crushing volume. I turn it down. A cross breeze comes through a screen door into the living room/dining room, down the stubby narrow hallway and out the open door. She's wearing a white long sleeve button down cotton shirt over a blue tank top and green pants. Her belly is bubbled like a pregnant woman's, though she is not carrying anything, not even her urine, which flows almost freely from a "dropped bladder," she admits, embarrassingly, to me.

I'm wearing my new "Greetings from Cape Cod" T-shirt. The image of the Cape is yellow, surrounded by a sea blue background. I've got my orange swim trunks on, revealing my black and silver below-knee prosthesis, which is peg-leg shaped until just above the ankle. Then a backwards C shape drops or disappears into the rubber foot shell that hides where my Achilles heel would be. I'm barefoot on the blue-gray carpet.

We talked about the trip to Brockton we'd just made to see her sister Lois. After our visit, where she borrowed the Corcoran (my mother's great grandmother) Bible, we drove by the places her late brother Jim Hannan had lived with his family. We even took a drive by the old Samry Store at 1181 Main Street. My Grandpa Samry opened a butcher shop and grocery store in the Campello area of Brockton, not far from West Bridgewater, in the 1930s.

After the drive back from Brockton, we talk a little about the oil spill in the Gulf of Mexico, which is about an hour's drive from my house in Fairhope, Alabama. Sitting down on the sofa, I take the leg off to alleviate the pain I feel from a sore developing on my stump. I'm not looking at Mom, but I feel her watching. I unroll the black suspension sleeve, and lift the stump out of the socket. The stump dangles over the sofa, the cushions hidden under a blue slip cover.

She notices the sores immediately, a pinkish bubble and a bright raspberry on the inside of my stump and just below my knee.

"My doctor isn't sure if the sores are bone or tissue related," I say. I don't think it possible but her face turns a shade whiter. She does not see the other side of my leg, thankfully. It is much worse, and over scar tissue.

"I need a new leg but it doesn't make sense to start the fittings until they can figure out what the problem is." I tell her I've got an appointment with a pediatric orthopedist. His name is Dr. Nimit, short for Nimityongskul. Dr. Laura Sanspree, my primary doctor, says Nimit can identify stuff other doctors can't.

"Why?" my mom asks, as if she's suddenly acquired a reporter's tenacity.

"He's a pediatric orthopedist who holds clinics for children with orthopedic anomalies. Dr. Sanspree told me he's seen it all." She grabs her notepad and begins writing down the names of the doctors. I notice her notepad. The names of the doctors and the Red Sox line-ups and box scores are all printed. The heart attack, high blood pressure, two stents next to her heart, arthritis, and various hospital visits have crippled her hands, and her exquisite penmanship.

I tell Mom that after reading about a birth defect called PFFD, or proximal focal femoral deficiency, I began to wonder if that was what I had. I read about PFFD in *Poster Child*, a memoir by Emily Rapp, and based on the symptoms I read about, suspected that I, too, may have been misdiagnosed by doctors at Shriners Hospital in Springfield, Massachusetts. PFFD is a congenital bone and tissue disorder that causes hips, femurs, and lower legs to develop abnormally in the womb. The affected side is typically shorter and the body continues to grow unevenly. Hip, joint, kidney, and back problems can also occur. We don't know what happened to me, and as my body ages, I've become paranoid about some recent back and stomach problems.

"Dr. Nimit may be able to diagnose my condition from an examination."

"I took you to a clinic in Hyannis shortly after you were born," Mom recalls, referring to the Boston Children's Hospital clinic at Cape Cod Hospital.

"Nothing unusual happened when I was carrying you. I got sick of answering the same questions," she raises her voice, sensing a similar line of questioning from her son.

"They kept asking me if I took birth control pills. I never took birth control pills," she says, "until after you were born." Her voice cracks.

***

I still can't seem to find the best word or phrase to fit my situation of being born without part of my right leg. There are no words that accurately limn this condition. Today, we are lumped together as amputees. It's too complicated to respond accurately when people ask, "What happened to your leg?" I say, "It was a birth defect," or earlier in my life I'd say, "I was born like this." I think I answered a question with a question. "I was born like this?" Most kids didn't understand, and I wasn't comfortable enough with my own disability to make stuff up and lie about the condition. "Shark attack" would have been great, and I've told a few kids that these days, but I was far too serious about it when I was younger. I wanted to be accurate, even if they didn't understand. Never once did I imagine that I could make up stories about how I lost it. I was just passing down what I'd been told by my mother, Joan. Somehow over the years it had become an anchor of shame, something that weighed me down, yet it had the possibility to lift me up too.

Other ways I've described the leg are: "I wear a prosthesis," "I have an artificial leg," or "I've got a fake leg." The last was a favorite when I was a kid. No matter what I said, kids named me "cripple" or "peg leg."

***

There are lots of student interns from the University of South Alabama Medical School assisting Dr. Nimit during my visit. I clutch my records from Shriners as the nurse guides me into the exam room.

A black man in long dreadlocks, white doctor's jacket, and gray scrubs walks in, and introduces himself as Brad Taylor, a medical student. I notice his name is embroidered on his coat. He's a mocha-skinned man, handsome, late twenties, wearing New Balance sneakers.

"Would you mind if I take a look," he says. What he really means is that he wants to put his hands on me. Not in that way, but most orthopedic doctors are hands on; they feel for stuff. In my case I wonder if they know what they are feeling my stump for. It's not exactly anatomically correct. I'm used to doffing the leg; that's why I wear shorts. I pop it off for him. Literally, you hear a "pop" when the seal from the gel liner breaks. He presses, and then gently pokes the limb in a few places. Taylor's relaxed, at ease. The stump doesn't seem to bother him. This comforts me. I breathe.

I tell him I was a patient at Shriners Hospital and that there was not enough room on the form they gave me today to list surgeries. I grab the manila envelope with the records and sift to the back.

"This page is a summary of my surgeries." He starts taking notes. Perhaps he writes something like this: congenital defect, wears BK prosthesis full time, several surgeries, soreness over scars, no noticeable pain upon examination, says sores worsen as day goes on. Then he pulls the medical pages closer and begins writing again. Maybe he copies "1977 stump revision with resection of fibula, 1985 resection of right fibular head, and right tibia valgus osteotomy in 1987."

"Let's hope it's just some scar tissue causing you some problems." Yes, let's hope, I think to myself, but say, "Thanks."

"Dr. Nimit will be in shortly."

Another guy, green scrubs, calls himself Dr. Burkett, walks in. I have a reporter's ear and heard him as he stood outside the examining room flipping through my newly created chart. Since he didn't come in with the chart, I think he's shifty. I immediately distrust him. Does he think I'm a medical curiosity? I didn't leave my leg off to be on display for every student. He asks a few questions, similar to Taylor, but less interested, more matter-of-fact. It kills a few minutes of waiting.

Dr. Nimit is a slight man from Asia, Thailand actually. His black hair looks as if his buzz cut has gotten too long. It looks soft, like the red ends of a blooming bottle brush plant. His nostrils flare out as wide as his mouth.

Dr. Nimit says, "You are active, healthy, and have worn a prosthesis for a long time." He sounds like my fortune teller, not my physician.

He quickly gets down to business. "Normal knee function, hamstring, fibula head, distal end," he says softly, staring at the stump, and taking inventory. He pays extra attention to the sore area. Probing, pushing and squishing skin and bone.

I don't feel anything sha-arp," he adds, favorably. "Let's take a look at the X-rays." He looks at Taylor, who knows immediately that he should have ordered X-rays prior to Dr. Nimit coming in.

"Let's have some X-rays, okay, then I'll be back to take a look."

"PFFD," I blurt out just as he is turning to the door, "or hemimelia."

"If you have PFFD at all, it's a mild case, type one maybe? We'll X-ray your pelvis and your stump. Okay?"

"Yes, fine," I mumble.

A female technician comes in. I guess she saves her personality for the kids. Sitting there without my prosthesis on, stump extended like an erect penis, doesn't even get a rise out of her. I put my leg on fast because she's already walking out of the room, calling out over her shoulder, "It's this way to X-ray," not once looking back. She moves fast.

Back in the little room, waiting on the doctor.

"Alan, come out here," Dr. Nimit says—a request, not a demand. Taylor is beside him, putting my X-rays up in the hall, next to his office.

"You do not have PFFD," he says. "Look, the hips are normal." My mind hangs on that word, "normal," but it shouldn't have, because he's talking so fast I don't hear everything he says. He mentions something about the pelvic bone being different, but he attributes it to walking with a prosthesis.

He looks over at the leg X-ray and points to the area where I was experiencing some soreness.

"There is no structure problem here. When you have your new leg made you just need a little more relief around this surgical area. Look at this. The area around the condyles on both sides is smooth, smoother on the outside of your stump, and that's good."

After I gather my stuff and leave the room, I notice he is still explaining something to Taylor, so I say, "Doc, I've got one more question."

"Yes, Alan, what is it?"

"Is there a diagnosis for what happened? I mean, other than hemimelia and the fact that my right femur is shorter than the left."

"The birth defect itself was probably genetic," but he gives it a name, which he says and I don't fully understand. I ask him to write it down, so he does. Streeter's Dysplasia, and Amniotic Band Syndrome.

"You can Google it when you get home." I thank him sincerely, for the new words. I shake his hand again to express my excitement about the new terms to research, and add, "You don't know how helpful you've been."

"Alan," Dr. Nimit says, "if you have any more questions, don't hesitate to contact me."

***

I was born in 1967, with a birth defect, entering the world without a portion of a limb. Today, one in 2,000 babies born in the United States is missing all or part of a limb, according to the March of Dimes.

Most websites tell you birth defects are genetic. Genetic factors can include a mutation or change in a single gene. Environmental factors include mother's age and whether she's a smoker or drinker. The statistics show that low birth weight is attributed to smoking cigarettes. Birth defects occur more in babies born to mothers 35 years old and older. Ma was a smoker and a light drinker. Her pregnancy was normal and full term.

The Centers for Disease Control and Prevention website has lots of birth statistics and suggestions on how to have healthy babies. A subsection of the CDC site, called the National Center on Birth Defects and Developmental Disabilities, says this: "The cause of limb reduction defects is unknown." In fact, the causes of about 70 percent, or nearly three quarters, of birth defects are unknown.

In 2006 more than four million babies were born in the US Of those babies, approximately 122,000, 1 in 33, or 3 percent, were born with birth defects. A birth defect is defined as an abnormality of structure, function or metabolism, present at birth, that results in physical or mental disabilities or death. Thousands of birth defects have been identified and are the leading cause of death for babies in their first year of life. Most birth defects happen during the first three months of pregnancy.

The CDC now calls birth defects "congenital anomalies." In the most recent National Vital Statistics Report, Births: Final Data for 2006, underreporting of "birth defects" on birth certificates still persists.

Birth certificates are two-page PDFs now. Federal, state, and local governments have made great strides in trying to document birth defects on paper, but the problem of underreporting continues.

***

I have no military heroism, no great story to tell about a motorcycle crash, or a severing of a limb between a moving train and iron tracks. Lost leg, leg loss, and amputee are just a few of the ways to describe my condition. None seem accurate. I didn't lose my leg because I never had all of it, nor did I misplace it. One legged-ness implies that I've only got one leg.

I've got two, but one is incomplete. I like "leg in absentia," and it sounds romantic, but I'd still need to give an explanation. One writer recently described herself with one and a half legs.

Statistically, I'm a congenital amputee. It sounds like an oxymoron to me. I wonder what my birth certificate and announcement would say today. We know so much more than we did forty years ago, but that doesn't mean parents are willing to share the news of a defect, or the cause of it. The birth announcement is supposed to be a celebration of life.

Reflecting back on Gould's essay, "The Creation Myths of Cooperstown," I believe that society has evolved in how they identify people with limb loss and birth anomalies. In my lifetime, I've heard defects described as oddities, malformations, mutants, abnormalities, mistakes of nature, monsters, monstrosities, freaks, and mistakes God made. While I've been limning my disability and trying to find out "what happened" when I was born, society has been changing how they perceive people with limb loss. The people I meet are more accepting, more openly curious, and more knowledgeable about prosthetics. Like the game of baseball, I like to think I've evolved along with the culture. When I was a kid, I thought Abner Doubleday invented baseball. Now, I know the game evolved from many childhood stick-and-ball games.

Gould writes, "We yearn to know about origins, and we readily construct myths when we do not have data (or we suppress data in favor of legend when a truth strikes us as too commonplace)." My birth defect was suppressed for the opposite reason. It was uncommon. And yet, the myth, or omission, has some truth to it because there often is no data for parents and physicians as to the origins of a genetic anomaly.

In connecting baseball, humanity, and God, Gould writes, "The hankering after an origin myth has always been especially strong for the closest subjects of all – the human race." Tracing my story back to its beginning and through the surgeries, I feel ambivalent about the past. I find no comfort in explaining "born without" or "amputee" to people who want to know what happened. But I still tell them. I understand and accept the scientific words that explain my birth defect. It's been 41 years since the amputation that took the end of my stump for a better-fitting prosthesis. I've still not found the personal language to explain that loss, so I continue to search for the words to match the feelings of being a born amputee.

***

"Nobody gave me any answers," my mom says, recalling it as if it happened yesterday. "The doctors didn't know what to do. I didn't know what to do." A mother not knowing how to care for her son, her fifth child, seems unnatural. Having no answers from those who are supposed to know can be overwhelming, so I lean in and give her a hug, and say "Ma, taking me to Shriners was the best thing you did for me."

Bert Shepard

In the photograph, Bert Shepard is in his baseball uniform with his right pant leg rolled up. He's wearing a joints-and-corset, or thigh lacer prosthesis. Before Shepard joined the military in 1942, he played minor league ball. He was a pitcher and utility fielder for the Bisbee Bees in the Arizona-Texas League before joining the Army Air Force. After completing fighter pilot training in 1944, he was sent to Europe.

"In early May, we leveled off a field, laid out a diamond and started practice," Shepard remembered. Games were scheduled to start May 21. That same day turned out to be his 34th and final mission.

Shepard's P-38 Lightning was shot down by anti-aircraft fire. The plane crashed into the ground at 380 MPH. Enemy fire ripped through Shepard's leg and foot and he lost consciousness from the deep gash in his head. German Luftwaffe First Lieutenant Ladislaus Loidl, a physician, saved him from a bunch of irate farmers. He'd crashed into their crops. Years later, when Shepard met Loidl again, Loidl said he went through a lot of German brass to save Shepard's life. Shepard's right leg was amputated below the knee and he was transferred to Stalag IX-C, a prison camp in Central Germany. It was there that he met Doug Errey, a Canadian medic and fellow POW. Errey crafted Shepard's first artificial leg.

After a POW exchange, Shepard returned to the US walking on the same leg Errey had made. Once stateside, Shepard entered the Walter Reed Army Medical Hospital. The military had already begun experimenting with making artificial legs out of aluminum.

While still at Walter Reed he met Robert Patterson, Undersecretary of War. Patterson was impressed with the returning veteran's attitude about playing baseball again, so he talked to Clark Griffin, owner of the Washington Senators, and Shepard got a chance to try out for the team.

He reported to the Senators' camp on March 14th. Two weeks later, he signed on as a pitching coach and pitched well in an exhibition game against the Norfolk Naval Training Station. Then Shepard pitched four innings in a War Relief Fund Game on July 10 against the Brooklyn Dodgers.

George Case, a former teammate of Shepard's, remembered Bert as being "pretty damn good." Case, a former outfielder, said that since Walter Reed was near Griffin Stadium, "We'd have a couple of amputees at every game. They'd see Bert throw batting practice."

A camera crew showed up to practice one day. The newsreel captures Shepard and one-armed outfielder Pete Gray of the Cleveland Browns in action. Shepard is in the dugout pulling his sock up over his prosthesis. He's bending and straightening the leg for the camera. He's shown running the bases, running in place, and fielding grounders from the mound and throwing the ball to first base.

On August 4, 1945, with two outs in the fourth, down 14-2, Shepard was called in from the Griffin Park bullpen in a game against the Boston Red Sox. The crowd was full of suits, hats, a few closed umbrellas in shades of gray, brown and black. The grass was a faded green amidst the afternoon D.C. humidity. The rosin bag looked like a dirty snowball.

Shepard wore number 34 with the red S on the front and a W on his hat. His walk to the mound was both an early trip to heaven and a potential flashback to the war.

"If I would have failed, then the manager says, 'I knew I shouldn't have put him in with that leg.' But the leg was not a problem, and I didn't want anyone saying it was," Shepard remembered. The bases were loaded.

Although Shepard's leg clicked at every straightening of the knee, the new joints and corset or thigh lacer leg alleviated most pressure on the end of the stump. The corset around the thigh was tied tightly using parachute cord with metal eyelets punched out of the leather every half inch or so.

He toed the rubber with the good leg, his left. Blocking out the wound, the war, and worry was tough, but the warm-up tosses felt good. The first batter stood in: right-handed batter George "Catfish" Metkovich. Shepard put his weight back on the good leg, glove belt-high, ball back, release. Snap! The umpire was motionless. Ball one.

"I struck out Metkovich to get us out of it," Shepard remembered triumphantly.

In that August game, Shepard faced 20 batters, recorded 16 outs, and completed the game. He allowed one run on three hits, struck out two, walked one, hit a batter, and had two clean fielding assists for outs. At the plate, batting from the left side, he went 0 for 3. He grounded into a double play and struck out.

After a series of operations on his residual limb, Shepard never got another chance to play in the major leagues. He played and coached in the minor leagues for nine years and in 1954 went to work as an engineer for IBM and Hughes Aircraft. Shepard discounted his limitations during an interview with the *Associated Press* in 1990: "I was the type of person who never overrated my opponents. They've got two legs and two hands, the same as me."

Seventy-three seasons have passed since Shepard played for the Washington Senators. His record as the only player to wear an artificial leg in a Major League Baseball game remains unbroken.

Peter Stuyvesant: America's First Peg-Legged Leader

Ask any New Yorker about Peter Stuyvesant and you're likely to get a story. Not about the man, but about his grave, where he lived, or the neighborhood named after him.

Stuyvesant (1611-1672) was the Director General for the Dutch West India Company trading colonies in New Amsterdam and the Caribbean and he governed from the island of Manhattan from 1647 until 1664. He was a major figure in the early history of New York City. His 17th century peers included Governor William Bradford of Plymouth, Governor John Winthrop of Boston, and William Berkeley of Virginia. Of these early Atlantic settlements, Stuyvesant governed over the most diverse group of people on the tip of Manhattan for 17 years and then nearly vanished into obscurity. Colonial historians have virtually ignored him. Scholarly journal articles are devoid of Stuyvesant references. Admittedly, he was a tyrant and an anti-Semite during his rule on behalf of the Dutch West India Company, but as the first disabled leader in America in a world that celebrates individualism, and powerful men, Stuyvesant warrants a more prominent place in colonial history.

Caribbean Promotion and Amputation

On Curaçao, Stuyvesant's duties included overseeing the trade of sugar, salt, dyewood, tobacco, horses, and copper. It is likely that around this time Stuyvesant would have heard of or perhaps met and traded with the famous peg-legged privateer and fellow countryman Cornelius Jol. In fact Jol and Stuyvesant had the same employer: the Dutch West India Company.

After three years as a supplies officer, Stuyvesant was successful in his dealings with suppliers, traders, couriers, and privateers and for his dedication to company profits.

While Director General of the Islands of Curacao, Stuyvesant in March of 1644 attempted to take the island of St. Martin back from the Spanish. The force of 300 men threw up a low wall facing the fort and cannon were mounted on the wall. Stuyvesant climbed onto the wall to raise the Dutch flag and the Spanish fired. The cannonball hit him in the right leg, putting him out of action before the fighting even started. It took nearly three hundred years, but historian Kessler found a letter Stuyvesant wrote to the company that identified which leg he lost. "[The Attack] did not succeed as well as I had hoped, no small impediment having been the loss of my right leg."

The news of his amputation was relayed to his friend John Ferret, who had served under him in Curaçao and was now in Amsterdam. Ferret, who thought it was a noteworthy event, wrote the following poem titled, "On the Off-shot Leg of the Noble, Brave Heer Stuyvesant, Before the Island of St. Martin."

> What mad thunder ball comes roaring toward your leg
> My dear Stuyvesant, and causes your collapse?
> The right pillar that used to support your body
> Is that crushed and stricken off this way in one blow...
> You presented too fair a mark-O! much too cruel chance!
> My Stuyvesant, who falls and tumbles on his bulwark,
> Where, like a dutiful soldier, he taunted the enemy,
> To lure him into the field, on the island of St. Marten [sic].
> The bullet hit his leg; the rebound touches my heart. . .
>   (Shorto 152-153)

It seems appropriate that Stuyvesant was a staunch Calvinist because he, like anyone else in the 1600s, places his fate of surviving an amputation in God's hands. Medicine in the 17th century was placed into two categories: physicians who were university-trained and surgeons who were trained through apprenticeships with barbers. Barber surgeons, as they were known, performed amputations. However, they were more concerned with "trimming of hair than they were with operations." Membership in barber surgeon guilds required exams, but poor performance only meant a second exam taking or a payment of a fine which guild officers encouraged. These surgeons served on the ships and in the Dutch trading settlements in the Indies. John Woodall, the surgeon general of the English East India Company, writes in 1611 of the fate that awaited those facing amputations. "If you be constrained to use your saw let first your patient be well informed of the imminent danger of death by the use thereof. Let him prepare his soul as a ready sacrifice to the Lord by earnest prayers...and help from the Almightie and that heartily. For it is no small presumption to dismember the image of God."

Kessler, a medical doctor, points out that the cannon did not sever Stuyvesant's leg. The shot simply crushed it, resulting in compound fractures of the bones (tibia and fibula) below the knee, and requiring amputation. Kessler provides examples of the amputation procedure done during that time. They were called guillotine amputations. They consisted of a circular cut through the skin and soft tissues down to the bone. After the bone was sawed through, a large open wound remained. Bleeding was controlled by cauterization with hot irons or boiling oil. Anesthetics consisted of drinking large amounts of liquor. The wound would have to be dressed often and the scar would take 8 to 10 weeks to close. As if that was not painful enough, the amputee had to deal with the effects of the climate. In his diary of 1751, British surgeon John Knyveton wrote, "that it is almost always fatal to amputate a limb or digit in these Isles (in the Caribbean Sea)...and patient's condition ... soon sinks to rally no more." Stuyvesant, the thirty-four-year-old son of a Calvinist minister and a rising leader in the West India Company, refused to die. Despite the pain, both real and imagined (phantom pain), he continued to supervise the company's slave, horse, and salt trade operations from his bed.

Recovery, Leg Fitting, and Early Prosthetic History

He sailed for the Netherlands and stayed with his sister Anne Bayard's family in Alphen, near Rotterdam. He was nursed back to health by Judith Bayard. During his recovery, Stuyvesant's masculinity was challenged. Large quantities of wine were wagered between Stuyvesant and his future brother-in-law, who didn't believe Stuyvesant had the courage to propose marriage. John Ferret wrote another poem that he would never consummate the marriage. Stuyvesant shot back in protest and defended his manhood by responding that the lady he desired would "occupy this bed." He and Judith Bayard were married August 13, 1645. Although the chronological references are sketchy, it appears that he married Judith Bayard before he wore a peg leg. For disability historians, the fact that he was married prior to his peg leg is significant because despite his long recovery, his attitude about his future remained strong and he was able to convince a woman to be his wife.

The telling of his peg leg fitting is only accorded a few phrases in most biographical and historical book sources on Peter Stuyvesant and the New Netherlands. Sources documenting his leg, specifically what it actually looked like, have been absent. Charles Gehring and others before him have done tremendous work translating the records of the Dutch beginnings of New York. However, what the research offers regarding his peg leg is blurred between accounts of his recovery in the Netherlands, and his arrival in the New World. In cobbling together the sources, Peter Stuyvesant was "fitted with a peg leg" and "he decorated his leg with a silver band." There is not as yet any academic evidence of what the leg looked like beyond that description. Even the nickname "Old Silver Leg" has questionable origins. It's unfortunate that before attempts were made to accurately depict Stuyvesant's leg, children's authors and illustrators began taking too much artistic license to portray and paint a peg as they imagined it. The upside down double plunger with gold nails is perhaps the most realistic, despite the gold nails rather than silver band. The pock-marked peg isn't even comic book quality, and then there is the peg in a painting that looks more like a table leg. No two depictions of Stuyvesant's peg are alike. However, prosthetic leg history has been traced back 6,000 years, with the first 5,800 offering painfully slow progress, little innovation, and great designs with limited use. Of course, until the 19th century, only the wealthy could afford prosthetic devices.

The first prosthetic leg dates back to between 3500 and 1800 BC. The Rigveda, an ancient Indian poem, tells of Warrior-Queen Vishpla, who loses her leg in battle. A leg dated from 300 BC was made of a wood core, bronze shim, and leather straps. Between 1600 and 1800 the bulky and heavy prosthetics designed and built during the previous 2,000 years for appearance gave way to limbs being made for more common use. War, then as today, was the reason behind advances in amputations and prosthetic legs. Sources for prosthetic leg development came from numerous professions and trades including physicians, carpenters, shipbuilders, artisans, and watchmakers. The most renowned of all is Ambroise Paré, a barber-surgeon and prolific writer of the late 1500s. Suspension, or how the artificial leg stays attached to the stump or residual limb, created most of the problems for leg makers.

Ancient cultures used a simple crutch as a prosthetic, and then prosthetic legs developed and became a modified crutch or peg to free hands for other uses. Later, cloth rags were added to cushion the bottom of open socket legs and provided comfort to the distal tibia and fibula and produced better motion.

An undated design shows a pelvic belt attached to a wooden post that runs along the outside of the thigh to provide suspension, with a cushion inside the socket where the knee rests. Pieter Verduyn, introduced the first non-locking, below-knee prosthesis, referred to today as the joint corset or thigh lacer because the leather corset bears your weight and is supported by joints or two large external metal hinges on the sides of the corset that attach to the lower part of the leg socket. The socket for the residual limb below the knee was also lined with leather and the peg had a copper shell and even had a wooden foot. Innovation, invention, and evolution of limbs were continuous and ever changing. The records so far have been silent on details of Stuyvesant's peg leg, but it's likely that Stuyvesant's leg had characteristics of each of the above-mentioned peg legs.

One theory is that perhaps the knee-length knickers popularized by the Dutch were fastened below the cup socket and this provided suspension to hold the leg on. Or perhaps he wore the pelvic belt, which rested below his pantaloons and was unseen by the public that would have, like today, stared at the peg protruding from below his knee. Kessler states that Stuyvesant "had been fitted for the wooden leg he wore the rest of his life." It's likely that the wooden part held up, but the leather and any other movable parts would have needed maintenance and repair. As the General, it was likely that he did not take care of such things personally. More than likely one of his 50 or so slaves was entrusted to make sure the limb operated properly. It's also possible that on his return trip to face charges of surrendering New Amsterdam to the English, he could have been fitted for a new prosthesis. Kessler noted that "had he lost his knee, he would have used a crutch afterward instead of using an artificial limb." Children's books and statues in New York and New Jersey depict Stuyvesant using a cane, but no biographical data states conclusively or even indirectly that Stuyvesant ever used a crutch or a cane as a walking aid.

New Amsterdam, North America

Fate seemed to smile on Stuyvesant because just as he walked in to offer his services, company officials were looking to replace Willem Kieft as Director General. Rewarding Stuyvesant for his service and disability, they appointed him Director General of New Netherland and all the Dutch Caribbean interests in 1646. Stuyvesant was the first and only man the company appointed to oversee all North American and Caribbean Dutch interests.

New Amsterdam began as a fur trading post, not a colony like the English colonies to the north in New England and to the south in Virginia. Stuyvesant's job was all the more difficult as New Amsterdam was by all accounts America's first melting pot, consisting of numerous religions and nationalities. Father Isaac Jogues, a Jesuit missionary from Canada, provides a detail of the island in 1646, just a year before Stuyvesant arrived. "On the Island of Manhate, and in its environs, there may well be four or five hundred men of different sects and nations: the Dutch General (Kieft) told me that there were men of eighteen different languages."

Stuyvesant came to New Amsterdam with his wife, Judith, who was four months pregnant at the time they arrived in the East River on the *Great Crow* in May 11, 1647. His arrival in Manhattan was quite an occasion. The coming of the new leader was such a cause for celebration that the four-cannon salute blasted until the entire gunpowder supply was used up. The newly appointed Director General of New Amsterdam could see certain familiar landmarks on the island of Manhattan, which served as the capital of the trading settlement and fledgling colony. The church steeple and windmill within the walls of the fort offered familiar symbols of the Fatherland. The Fort, Stuyvesant later recalled, upon closer inspection looked "more a molehill than a fortress." He was rowed to shore amidst cheers from traders, settlers, and company employees.

As the boat landed, Stuyvesant's small sunken eyes and bulbous, hook-nosed face, came into focus. Draped with a breastplate and sword at the hip, Stuyvesant would have commanded attention as he stepped off the boat. Once he stepped onto land, people would have noticed an unnatural gait and that his rigid militaristic frame was supported by a peg leg. All eyes in the crowd would have stared long and hard at that leg, curious and perhaps even a little afraid of such a strange device.

The Last Peg Leg

The first time I saw him, I was stopped at the traffic light at the crossroads of Fairhope Avenue and Section Street in Fairhope, Alabama. The man, in his early 60s, rail thin and with a full white beard, walked towards the landmark green clock, made in Fairhope several decades ago by the Emperor Clock Company. I was in a car, stopped for the red light, as he walked in front of my hood. This guy wore shorts and walked with a wooden peg leg. He walked deliberately but quickly. He glanced in my direction with steely blue eyes and I gave a nod. It was not just the sight of him passing in front of my car, but the distinct sound that peg leg made on pavement. The tapping of a baseball bat on a hard surface quickly came to mind, but the peg had a much deeper and richer ring to it. He moved very swiftly to the brick sidewalk on the corner with the clock, and I drove toward the pier. I had moved here from Cape Cod just before Hurricane Katrina in 2005, but now I began to wonder whether the time on the clock, and in this town, had stood still.

A few months later I saw him again, walking in Walgreen's Pharmacy on Greeno Road. He had a steady, deliberate short-legged pace, but it was awkward because the man's frame was not centered over his legs. I suspected it was difficult to walk on tile, a smooth surface that provided no grip, with a peg that was only one or two inches in diameter, and that he was adapting with a different stride. Being the curious type, and since I was a reporter for the *Fairhope Courier*, I began thinking of a possible story. I left the store to go talk to him.

We introduced ourselves to each other. His name was Bob. We began looking at each other's below-knee prosthetic legs. They could not have looked more different, but because we shared the same condition we probably talked about 15 minutes. His leg was something from what I thought was a bygone era. I was in high school more than twenty years ago the last time I'd seen a wooden peg leg in action. In the middle of the Walgreen's parking lot with the foot of my prosthetic leg on the bumper of his 1980s Jeep Comanche pick-up, we started talking about our prosthetic legs. The conversation didn't begin with the typical "What happened?"

"What kind of set-up is that?" Bob asked, looking at my prosthesis carefully.

"This is a carbon fiber post and socket with a College Park Trustep foot with a multi-axial ankle. I wear a gel liner over my stump that fits into the carbon fiber socket." My limb was attached with a neoprene suspension sleeve. His peg had no moving parts except for the strap which secured his below-knee prosthesis above his knee.

"I made the peg myself," Bob said in a soft yet distinctly Southern voice. The leg was smooth, not adorned with anything and the light brown wood had a clear coat of varnish or stain over it, glistening in the spring Alabama sun. The peg tapered as it extended past the calf area to the ankle. He unbuckled the strap, leaned on his truck, and doffed the peg. His stump ended just before mid-calf, and his residual leg was the shape of a normal leg. He wore just two thin socks and it amazed me that he didn't have any sores on his stump after all day in a wooden boat of a socket.

Swapping details of legs reminded me of the scene from *Jaws* when Quint and Hooper are on the boat in pursuit of the Great White, telling shark stories, and they decide "to drink to our legs." Bob was proud of the leg he made and said he continued to improve upon his leg making. As a hobby, he said he was building a car from the frame up. I didn't doubt him, and in some ways I admired his know-how. I rolled down my suspension sleeve and lifted my stump from the socket.

"Despite all this new gel technology, my bony, malformed stump still gets skin irritations and causes fitting problems for prosthetists." Here I was, a product of the era of machines and technology, standing on a two-year-old leg that cost about $10,000 that somebody else made, while in front of me stood a slightly hunched-over man in T-shirt, cutoff jeans, and paint-spattered white canvas shoes who began telling me he made his own leg and said it cost him about fifty bucks.

"I'm looking for a new strap," he bragged, dropping his jaw awkwardly, "that costs less than two dollars."

I never considered Bob for a story at the time because our conversation seemed too personal, and I never mentioned I was a reporter. I saw him one other time, but we only exchanged short greetings. In January 2009, I began thinking about this man and set out to learn more about him. Questions continued to resonate with me as I began researching the history of prosthetic legs and their wearers in America. More details of his life, his leg, and why our paths crossed seemed important.

When I began asking friends and acquaintances around town about the man with the peg leg in Fairhope, many said they had seen him. However, none had spoken to him. A few people referred to him as Ahab, the whale-ivory peg-legged captain in *Moby Dick*. At first, I thought this was an insult. Then I read *Moby Dick* and began craving a peg of my own. I immediately appreciated and identified with Melville's character. Ahab is a tragic hero: a mythical character that I admire. I rooted for Ahab, brooding on the deck with his peg cradled in its auger hole. His monologue to the crew in the chapter "The Quarter-Deck" was the stuff of legend. I loved the scene so much I read it as part of a presentation I gave at the

Fairhope Museum of History. "Aye Starbuck, aye, my hearties all around," I told the tea drinkers that day as if I were gathering them around the main-mast. I didn't just say the lines, I felt them: my leg was "half-revolving in his pivot hole."

I continued my search for the peg-legged man of Fairhope, whom I only knew as Bob. I saw his truck on several occasions parked in a driveway near my house. I vowed to stop in some time and inquire, but before I could the truck was gone.

An appointment with my prosthetist Jeff Hendrix of Hanger Prosthetics and Orthotics in Fairhope revealed a few more clues.

"I saw him over a year ago," Hendrix said. He had made a plaster cast of Bob's stump so the man could use the mold to begin carving the socket of a new peg leg.

"I'll call the phone numbers I have for him and see if he wants to talk with you, Alan," offered Jeff's office assistant, Melissa, in her Mississippi smoker's rasp.

I was too late to interview Robert M. "Bob" Youens. He died on November 6, 2007, from diabetes complications. Bob was only 62 and, sadly, Youens' mother outlived him, according to the obituary in the *Fairhope Courier*. It turns out he was from Chickasaw, Alabama, which is just outside of Mobile, and had served in the Navy, as did my father. His peg leg was made of teak. Youens told Hendrix that he wore a modern prosthesis after his leg was amputated but began making his own after he was unable to afford health insurance. (That story is suspect, too, as my friend, Peggy – yes, "Peg" for short – had a friend tell her that Youens began making his own legs because the newer legs never fit well.)

The obituary said Youens was "known for his mechanical ingenuity" and even held a patent for an auto part he developed. In a testament to his mechanical innovation, Hendrix said Youens had installed hand levers between the front seats of his British car that worked as a hand brake that allowed him to drive a standard shift without having to use his peg.

When I think back on our brief encounters, Youens probably wouldn't have minded being referred to as the infamous captain of the *Pequod*. A smart, innovative guy, Youens rejected the plastic and carbon fiber prosthetic world, and with whale bone no longer an option, stayed with wood.

5. Fiction

N. "Why, I knowed a one-legged whore one time. Think she was takin' two bits in a alley? No, by God! She's gettin' half a dollar extra. She says, 'How many one-legged women you slep' with? None!' she says. 'OK,' she says. 'You got somepin' pretty special here, an' it's gonna cos' ya half a buck extry.' An' by God, she was gettin' 'em too."

Mirror Lake, not far from Mount Hood, and east of Stumptown, also known as Portland, Oregon

Undertow

O. "The cure for anything is salt water: sweat, tears, or the sea."

I walk in the unceasing wind-driven drizzle at Marconi Station in Wellfleet, Massachusetts. My lined windbreaker is about as useful as a seersucker shirt. The 100-foot bluffs on the Atlantic side of Cape Cod are what Henry David Thoreau called "the bare and bended arm of Massachusetts," which stretches from Monomoscoy, Chatham, to Race Point, Provincetown.

As I approach the area, it's not the same. It's been 25 years. There used to be a sloping beach-grassed dune with wires and cement stumps and salt-cured timber. The sea has claimed most of it. A piece of lumber lay on the ground. Only the outstretched Atlantic lies beyond the metal fragments and guy wires on the ground. One hundred years ago, Guglielmo Marconi sent his first transcontinental wireless message from England to this place. The world, just as Marconi predicted, is getting smaller.

I was returning home. The place you think of when you're middle-aged, living in a new place, and have the opportunity to reflect on the direction, or the lack of direction, in your life. I knew there was more than I could remember about the places we went to when I was a kid. In middle age, I began to feel something was missing. Was it homesickness, nostalgia, or being born without my leg? My quest to connect with my earliest senses of self could only be found in the place where I grew up. I went home to Cape Cod; to Brewster, and Eastham to remember the memories of childhood and to recall the landscapes and seascapes from a child's eyes.

My Samsung flip phone vibrates.

"Are you alright?" my sister Lynne asks.

"I'm fine," I say unconvincingly.

I park the Kia Sorrento in front of the parking lot at Cahoon Hollow Beach because I see a familiar sign. "Local Sticker Parking Only," it cautions. Unlike Marconi, Cahoon offers a break in the 120-foot bluff so you can walk down a steep sandy incline to get to the Atlantic.

From my seat on a split rail fence at the top of the bluff, they look like a pack of black seals. Surfers in wetsuits a football field from the shoreline. Thoreau walked the entire outside arm of the Outer Cape. The people, rugged, careworn and genuine, were what he liked best. It's still a windy, barren, unforgiving place and that's why I return. It's consistent. The Atlantic still rises and falls twice a day.

The water, according to my Wampanoag friend John "Bunny" Lopez, comes from the "Creator." When I was young, I worshiped water like the Wampanoag. Cape Cod Bay, the Atlantic, and Flax Pond were my Trinity.

I gaze at the sea. The waves have a rhythm, a beat. They come in sets and they break differently within those sets. If you want to know about a wave or your past, watch the water.

* * *

My father's new summertime friend John Sokerkowski had a house at the end of Prell Circle in Brewster. The two men used to curse themselves over Schaeffers and shots of Seagram's V.O. Not over jobs, but the fact they were two Polacks who married Irish women who sometimes acted as stubbornly as Maureen O'Hara in *The Quiet Man*.

It was Mr. Sokerkowski's idea to have his daughter take swimming lessons. Mary Sokerkowski was my age, 9. The dads were both Navy men, but I never saw either of them actually swimming. They waded, or stood around in knee-deep water with beer cans resting on their bellies. Frank and John hated the phrase "dumb Pollack," but "cheap Pollack" was a compliment so they agreed that I would teach Mary how to swim.

A few mornings later, my brother Matt and I went to the beach after he got off night crew at Stop and Shop in Orleans. He drove his blue 1970 Chevy half-ton with four-wheel drive to Cahoon Hollow Beach. He took a nap on the beach waiting for friends to join him later in the morning. Lynne and Mary got dropped off later on and walked down the steep sand and walked to the right until they came to the "ship skeleton," or the wooden ribs of a ship sticking up through the sand at low tide. There were three or four ribs sticking out of both sides. The keel was so thick you could only see the top of it, the rest lay buried under the sand.

"Alan will be sitting on the beach with Matt, or in the water to the right of the surfers," Lynne remembered telling Mary as they walked the wet sand closest to the shore, her footprints pressing water away, lightening the color of the sand.

"He thinks it's his break, but I think people are afraid of him, so they leave him alone." As Lynne talked to Mary, she kept calling her brother "different." His face was carved out of a window of hair, a style resembling the label of a Dutch Boy paint can. He had blue eyes and his nose fit his face, not too big or small.

"I am city-white," Mary said. Lynne heard her over the constant roar of the surf.

***

I wade out to where the larger waves were breaking. I can already feel the push and pull of the water around my thighs.

The feel of the undertow, or the current of water beneath the surface after the waves break, is going to be a force today with the high surf. My nuts are in my stomach at the shock from the 62-degree water temperature in July. Once I recuperate from that, I dive head first into the face of a wave. My heart, no matter how I get in, pounds right out of my chest. It takes a few minutes of leaning into a few oncoming waves to slow my heart rate to a gallop. By August, the water becomes just a bone-chilling 68 degrees.

I crouch down with my chest facing the shoreline and I look back over my right shoulder to see a nice five-footer breaking into a small curl. I turn. Swim hard. It's got me. I push my arms straight out like a diver, palms together as the wave carries me around the torso. My shoulders, arms, and head are poking out from the face of the wave. The silence makes me feel happy. My body is surfing a wall of water that in this depth would bust most boats in two. My mind is blank. The water envelops me. I ride for 40 yards and instinctively know when to start holding my breath. The wave you have known intimately rejects you, and pummels you under into the sand and pebbles. I'm in the soup. Some call it the washing machine where the undertow tries to keep you from surfacing. It's got me. Spin. Shake. Roll. Rinse. Amazingly, I know which way is up, but the undertow can carry you helplessly back to where the big waves break. I learned from Diane Masterson, the lifeguard for Flax Pond at Nickerson State Park in Brewster. "Stay cool," she said, "panicking makes things worse." Of course experience, being caught in the grinding surf, helps the most. Don't fight the undertow, let it carry you, and it will, eventually, let you go. I'm not afraid when I'm in the water. I kept swimming in the ocean even after *Jaws* came out.

The undertow lets me loose. I stand up in waist-high water considering another ride. As I glance at the shore, and catch my breath, I see a wave from a girl I don't recognize wearing a white T-shirt and denim cutoffs. It must be Mary. Lynne said she was coming down today. I recognize Lynne's round face, black hair and hazel eyes staring back at me. I swim back to shore quickly.

***

Lynne remembered Mary staring at the ship skeleton, waves gently lapping the mostly buried and massive keel. I was standing in waist-high water.

"How big are the waves?" Mary asked.

When I was bodysurfing, Lynne remembered pointing to me and telling Mary that I looked like the front of a torpedo sticking out of the wave, until the wave closed over me. Mary lost sight of me for what Lynne thought was a couple of minutes.

I stood up awkwardly and moved toward the shore in a herky-jerky motion. I dove under and came up swimming, face down in the froth and foam. When I stood up again they could see the orange board shorts that I'd taken from a box of my brother David's things that he'd packed away in the basement before he joined the Marine Corps.

"Mary thought you were hopping because you hurt yourself," Lynne said. Instinctively, Mary took a few steps into the water to help. Then she stopped. When I looked at Mary, she was staring at me. I hopped to the towel, which was hung over one of the ship's ribs, just a few yards away.

Mary looked at Lynne, back at me, leaning on the inner part of the curved rib, then back at Lynne.

"My dad wants me to take swimming lessons from a kid without a leg!"

Lynne burst into a giggly girl laugh at John Sokerkowski's idea of a joke. She loved the man probably more than her own father because despite his jokes, he loved his daughters and he made sure they knew it. Lynne especially liked being in on the joke, but she quickly turned to Mary.

"He was born without part of his leg, but the only person who can swim better than me is Alan," Lynne told Mary. Her voice rode a wireless wave, above the heavy sound of the surf and just loud enough for me to hear.

6. Periodicals

P. "Reading is the creative center of a writer's life."

Wedding Day: March 16, 1991

To my bride: Susan Michele Samry

Gifts can cost a treasure,
So I submit to you these rhymes.
Writing them has been a pleasure
But they're a tiny fraction of our good times.

Thinking about the waves of memories and moments we
share,
Remember, have some patience, and always know I care.
Read these words and you will see, that for me
Every day with you is a happy anniversary.

Through the years our love has taken us near and far.
Going places together has become part of who we are.
Before we take that next drive, board the next plane,
Let's take some steps down memory lane.

Wow what a pair, your legs more powerful
than plutonium.
Over time, mine of wood, plastic, carbon fiber,
and titanium.
Climbing lighthouses from Highland
to California's Point Sur.
Turning twenty-one at Shriners, eating Abdow's Big Boy
Burger.

Sunrise at Nauset Beach, welcoming in the year's first day,
Watching the sun set into Monterey Bay, all those miles
away.
Touring Boston Harbor on a lighthouse cruise,
Or riding Giant Dipper on the boardwalk in Santa Cruz.

146

Friends and family at gatherings through the years
Weddings, funerals, graduations, big games, barbecues,
Wifflebar with brothers, sisters, nieces, and nephews
Tossing hats, high fives, and rice, letting fall the tears.

Swimming at Flax Pond in Brewster at Nickerson.
Panoramic hues of brown and orange, Grand Canyon
Dining at No. 9 Park, a table overlooking the Common.
Chinatown in San Francisco, and no it didn't taste like
chicken.
The Pacific from the Beach Chalet, now that was golden.

East Bound and Down, or, dun dun dun dun dun
are my favorite movies, you know the ones.
Yours is a chocolate factory tour full of fun.

Our beloved Red Sox, Bruins, and Patriots too,
Together we've shared the highs of Super Bowl wins
Triple overtime at Klydes, Edmonton's Peter Klima, boo,
The pitching duel at Camden Yards, Mussina versus
Clemens.
Drinking Sam Adams when it was still a microbrew,
how 'bout that Pizza Hut pie, Priazzo.
Sosa's three homers at Wrigley, biking along Lake
Michigan
Jacob Mordecai and Jada Josephine are given lots of
affection.

Cape Cod Bay with tidal pools so shallow
Body surfing in the cold Atlantic at Cahoon Hollow.
Getting to the head of the line at Lady Liberty
Teddy Bears with names of Cocoa and Smokey

Clothes hanging on the line at home and in Amish
Country.

Rhythms of euphoria:
Naomi's Mezuzah
The icy falls of Niagara
Sonic tater tots along the Redneck Riviera
Gazing in awe in Muir Woods at the mighty sequoia.

No matter where our travels take us
By dream, foot, car, plane, boat, or bus
From the White Mountains to the Rockies, so majestic
to the range of emotions gushin', as you listen to the lyric
I'll swear before angels never to be mean or cruel
If you forgive the anger, pettiness, crankiness from no
fuel.

Holding hands on the plane as we take to the air
Strolling the grounds of our county's fair.
Standing at Gettysburg, hallowed land
Soon we'll walk together on black sand
Impressionist paintings of Venice by Monet,
The world's collection at Boston's MFA

There is love in my heart every night.
When I look into your eyes by candlelight,
I'm happier still, simply hearing the hum of the
refrigerator
At our home on the road named after the Portuguese
Navigator.

(This poem first appeared as an advertisement in *The
Falmouth Enterprise*, March 16, 2004, on page five.)

$64.95 Buys Lifelong Dream for Resident

As a native Cape Codder, it seemed natural that I would take to the water, which I have, but last week I was able to break down a major barrier that had prevented me from wading into local waters.

I was born without a complete right leg, and although it posed a challenge to getting in and out of the water, it just meant leaving the artificial leg in the sand, hopping down the beach on one leg and into the water.

My parents, worried about my swimming capabilities, sought out several lifeguards willing to help at Flax Pond at Nickerson State Park in Brewster, who taught me how to swim at the age of four.

Growing up, I would spend the entire day at the pond, swimming or diving off my brother's rowboat or cruising from the deck of a neighbor's Sunfish sailboat.

The ocean proved more of a challenge, and because of the tidal flats, we did not frequent the bay beaches too often because even a kid gets tired after hopping several hundred yards just to reach the water.

The ocean side beaches and bigger waves are what I craved anyway. Playing in the sand was never an option; I was either body surfing or gliding on one of those white Styrofoam boards at Nauset Beach. Even seeing the movie *Jaws* did not stop me from going in the water.

As I grew up, I never lost my passion for swimming, but I swam less often because it became difficult to hop into the water, plus the stares could be downright unbearable.

149

Most times my disability was easily explained, but by my early 30s, hopping in and out of the water was no longer an option.

Through the miracles of the Internet, I found something that would allow me to take my prosthetic leg into the water.

It was ingrained in my mind from the get-go not to get the leg wet because the materials used in the construction of the limb were not waterproof.

There are limbs made for the water, but they are expensive and not covered by insurance.

On a recent Sunday, I found my sea legs.

I was skeptical to say the least, about a latex waterproof cover that would allow me to take an $11,000 limb into the water, and here is the best part, for only $64.95.

The Drypro arrived in the mail two weeks ago, just in time for the rain and cooler weather, which postponed my test.

My wife, Susan, came with me to John's Pond in Mashpee for moral support and as rescue personnel in case I took on water and sunk like the *Titanic*.

Now, I put this thing on over a slightly less expensive limb, and my wife announced that it looked like a giant condom, at which time several dirty jokes surfaced.

I took a few careful steps into the water, which was cool but nothing like the 65-degree water at Nauset.

I made sure to let the air out, per the only instructions.

Keep in mind that for my entire life I have always hopped into the water. For the first time I was doing what most take for granted, including tourists from Minnesota who have never seen the ocean. I waded, which proved to be a bonus that I had not fully realized, and it felt great.

For cautionary reasons, I chose not to dive in but leaned in like an orca sliding back in after it breaks the ocean's surface.

I swam, I kicked, I dove and in a more positive reference to the movie *Titanic* I was "on top of the world" and better yet, I wasn't sinking or even taking on water.

It was pure bliss, but I needed more, so it was a trip to Menauhant Beach in Falmouth for another dip for further testing.

I don't know how long this device has been on the market, but having overcome the limitation, I may someday fulfill a lifelong dream.

Surfing instructors wanted.

Contact sheet of photos taken by Dan Webb at
Menauhant Beach, East Falmouth, MA

The Gulf War

The news about the oil in the Gulf is spreading. There is a feeling of dread, depression, and impending doom as the first black tar balls stick to the white sand beaches at Gulf Shores, Alabama, on Friday, June 4. One's perceptions can vary depending on what one hears or sees. On my first day off from work after Memorial Day, my wife Sue and I decided to take the 45-minute ride to the Gulf of Mexico from our home in Fairhope, Alabama. I spent most of my life on Cape Cod and moved to Fairhope in 2005. In all that time I'd taken going to the beach for granted. I went to the Gulf to see for myself. I swim. I planned on swimming. Will it be safe to swim? I was pessimistic about what the future held for swimmers. I went to say goodbye to the sea, but for how long? I did not know.

I learned quickly that it's not "the ocean" here in LA (Lower Alabama), it's "The Gulf"—an important distinction to me when I moved here five years ago, but one that everyone is being forced to learn nationally from the Gulf Coast news reports from Louisiana to Florida.

On a partly cloudy morning with a high chance for showers, we took a left out of our subdivision off County Road 48. We passed the Fish River swimming hole at Bohemian Park. We snaked down County Road 9, then onto 98, then 65 South, admiring the seven-foot-high green corn stalks with beige bushy husks on acres and acres of farmland. Later, on 59, we saw traffic heading north away from the beaches. We took a left at The Hangout restaurant and bar on the Gulf with the backdrop of high-rise condominiums stretching east.

We see an AMECO caravan pulling into Gulf State Park Pavilion. The park serves as a base for the coastal cleanup company crews. We continue on to our favorite beach, Cotton Bayou, named for the inlet behind the stretch of Gulf in Orange Beach. The parking lot is slap full. We pull in where someone pulls out. A parking lot full of cars and trucks indicates tourists and locals alike are still heading to the beach.

Like the oil spill, part of me is manmade. I change into an older, below-knee prosthesis so I can get in and out of the water. I used to have what I called a "condom" that covered my prosthesis, but now I just wear an old leg at the beach. We carry our gear across the boardwalk over the sand dunes and fragile beach grass. There are hundreds of people on the beach.

The red flag is flying. NO SWIMMING! I'm not sure if that's due to the surf, which is pretty high today at two to four feet, or because of the incoming oil. Riptide, or what I call undertow, is also part of the red flag equation for swimmers.

"There are lots of people in the water," Sue says, as my rubber foot squeaks in the hot sand. There are kids of all ages and sizes. Some ride boogie boards, while others swim and splash. A few heads farther out bob in the wax and wane of the waves. Teenage girls turn their backs to oncoming waves. One guy moves his arms back, leans forward, and chest-thumps a wave.

"Yeah," I say, trying to process a surreal scene of beachgoers. The news reports and my own observations contradict.

A barge loaded with booms is anchored a few hundred yards offshore. A buoy tender spews black diesel from its stack as it heads into the wind. The breeze from the southwest carries the spent fuel northeast. There is no salt to taste today. The air is humid, petrol-ed. I'm breathing oil vapors. It reminds me of the garage smell from when I worked at Al Cormier's old Shell station on Route 151. It also reminds me a little of the smell in our basement in Falmouth when the heating oil tank was full.

We spread out our towel and sit down in the sand, which looks and feels the same way it did in April. An empty dolphin cruise boat passes by. A Coast Guard plane circles overhead. No one is parasailing. Banners towed by three different planes advertise Alvin's Island merchandise and Doc's Seafood restaurant platter. The guy next to me goes into the water to rinse sand off his Coca-Cola bottle.

A personal watercraft jets by, and I spot a red marker bobbing about 200 yards offshore near the surfer's break. "It's an oil monitor," Sue says.

"I'm going in," I announce, taking off my On the Water hat, shades, and Hendrix T-shirt. Sue gets up and walks the few feet to the water's edge; her feet are covered by the water.

"There's tar balls," she says over the mesmerizing sound of crashing surf. I get up to have a look. Melted chocolate—just like the reports. I prefer oil globs.

When a guy with a prosthesis walks in the water, people notice. Today, they don't. I do not feel stares or field questions from curious kids. Perhaps my leg has taken a back seat to our heightened awareness of this impending black doom.

I wade in a few steps and feel the cool rush over my leg. I continue through whitewater froth of the wave break. I jackknife as a chest-high wave approaches and I stumble at its power. I dive into the face of the next wave. Once past the breakers I float, prop my legs up, and stare at the skin-tone prosthetic foot minus the torn-off toes amidst an altering backdrop of charcoal clouds and Neptune blue water. I swim a few strokes to realign myself with Sue, still wading in ankle-deep ebb and flow.

Typically, this is a day to body surf waves. I do not want to have fun. I study the break and the sets from the shore and do so again in the Gulf. Several waves pass before one peaks over my head. I turn to the shore. The wave rests me gently in the shallows. The Gulf waves goodbye to me.

As we get in the car for the drive home, Sue says, "It feels like a war zone." I know what she means, because she says it just as a Coast Guard helicopter flies over our heads. We are waging another war for oil. Our insatiable need for oil is juxtaposed by our lofty goal to wean ourselves off it. BP is our new enemy, and the Gulf of Mexico is just our latest battleground. The tourists, cars, boats, and the planes overhead should serve as a reminder. We are all swimming in oil every day.

One Nation, Divisible

The subject of secession in the book, *Bye Bye, Miss American Empire: Neighborhood Patriots, Backcountry Rebels, and their Underdog Crusades to Redraw America's Political Map*, by Bill Kauffman got me to thinking on a larger scale about the importance of local people determining what's best for their own neck of the woods.

If we in Fairhope, Alabama, are "eccentric," as a city official claims because it was founded on the utopian principles of Henry George, and full of nudists, socialists, and worst of all artists, then crying jags for a new school district is just the tip of the iceberg. I'm a patriot to the core. I grew up loyal to Falmouth, Massachusetts, hometown of America-the-Beautiful songstress Katharine Lee Bates, and I have now clearly realized something in my new hometown is amiss. The ratings of our state and national representatives are at an all-time low. Wars for democracy against tribal factions, and out-of-control spending are undermining core values of American independence. The nation, or her respective states, is too big to be governed from one city.

Take a deep breath here and keep an open mind. Let's secede from the Union and form our own nation, or state. Treasonous, you say! Well, yes, and that's precisely what our nation's foundation rests upon. What are our other choices? Refusal to pay taxes equals an automatic go-directly-to-jail, so that's not an option. Secession means to withdraw from and it's not a new idea. In fact, its origin is in the Declaration of Independence, which states that England had "an absolute tyranny over these states." Now our federal and state governments wield all the power.

Today, there is no self-governance in Baldwin County because Montgomery and Washington make our decisions for us. Beyond that, they take our wealth and redistribute it throughout the state. I'm all for paying my share, but why are we paying more than our share? The Tea Party shouts reform, and I admire that and would join them if I thought that their movement could move mountains. The problem is that the federal and state governments are so big, they will simply swallow up the Tea Party over time by wearing it down and dividing it against itself, especially in a two-party system. Don't be fooled by the shift in power at the state and national level either. We've seen it before and it doesn't seem to matter who's in charge.

Our separation idea is not unique, as there have been other secession movements. It's true. There was secessionist talk in New England in 1804. Roughly a half century later South Carolina seceded and the War of Northern Aggression was on.

Please consider joining me in forming the new state, nation, or nation state of LA. In Lower Alabama, we'll take along whoever is willing to break away, including Mobile, Mobile County, West Florida, and any adjacent counties in Florida clear across to Mexico. Maybe we could become the Gulf States of America or the good ol' GSA. This area has been frontier territory for so long anyway that we should just break away. We've been under so many flags, isn't it time we had our own? Perhaps we could put in a large claim to BP since we'd have most of the Gulf coastline.

Our community could do just what hundreds of other nations have done when forming a new nation: use the United States Constitution, and the earlier, and some say better, Articles of Confederation as a template. Experts argue today that the US Constitution is more suited to smaller countries, and that's why no one here in America seems to be paying much attention to it anymore.

We don't need to look any further than Alabama's "proud" secessionist history. We can be inspired just cradling our buns in a porch rocker on the gray boards of the first White House of the Confederacy in Montgomery, Alabama. Jefferson Davis and Robert E. Lee, smart West Point graduates both, read William Rawle's textbook, *A View of the Constitution of the United States of America*, in 1825. It was in Mobile among the live oaks and tall pines on the campus of the University of South Alabama that I have learned about Reverend Henry Highland Garnet, a former slave and fake leg wearer, like myself, who was a radical abolitionist. He gave a sermon to Congress when it was a place for doing the nation's business and doubled as a religious congregation of more than 2,000 people. His sermon followed the passage of the 13th Amendment, abolishing slavery. He was the first black man to speak in Congress. Another Montgomery/Davis connection is worth mentioning here too.

Jefferson Davis's brother Joseph owned a large plantation at Hurricane, Mississippi. After the war, the elder Davis gave property to his plantation business manager and son, Benjamin and Isaiah Montgomery. Isaiah founded the all-black town of Mound Bayou, Mississippi. (For further study on the Civil War, come into my place of employment, the Fairhope Public Library, and feel free to browse our collection, all 129 volumes, of *The War of the Rebellion: A Compilation of the Official Records of the Union and Confederate Armies Prepared Under the Direction of the Secretary of War*, by Robert N. Scott. If you decide to take a look at the volumes, you'll be in mixed company. You may find yourself sitting between Canadian snowbirds and war re-enactor types straight out of *Confederates in the Attic*.)

The secession movements, Alta California and the Nation of Alaska, have been alive and dead, at the same time, since before the Civil War. Alta California was the brainchild of John Sutter, according to Kauffman's book. Before gold was even discovered at Sutter's Mill, Sutter fantasized about Alta California. His vision of a republic would not answer to Washington. I wish I could tell you in a few sentences about the Nation of Alaska. They are such an independent-minded people up there; they really don't seem to care what we do in the lower 48. John McPhee, most famous for his essay, "The Search for Marvin Gardens," pretty well summed up the Alaskan attitude when he profiled John Vogler in his book, *Coming into the Country*. "A roamer, a garrulous companion, a sort of cartoon Alaskan self-drawn," is what McPhee wrote, but Kauffman really captures the man and mantra of Alaskans. Vogler is the "Tundra Rebel," and a "fuck-you-I'll-do-it-my-way gold prospector."

Secession is a cultural issue, not a patriotic one. Conservatives, liberals, and independents are working together separately attempting to break away from Uncle Sam. Did you know that Vermont was a Republic that governed itself once? The Second Vermont Republic wants another crack at self-governance. There is no doubt that the South is beginning to look a lot like the rest of the United States too. The Holiday Inn Express, a Waffle House, or Cracker Barrel sits at the bottom of every exit ramp. We must defend local diversity against national conformity!

Can secession work?

What of currency, you say? Well, shinplasters worked for Fairhopians, and by gum, they oughta work for us too. In the early 1900s, the Fairhope Industrial Association created association scrip AKA shinplasters. They were accepted at the cooperative store and were used to pay teachers too. (I don't have the space to explain Fairhope's complicated yet colorful beginnings, so Google any of the key terms in this paragraph, or socialist movement, Fairhope Founder E. B. Gaston's "cooperative individualism," utopian community, or Familistére for more background.) Back then, the Single Taxers even used shinplasters to buy shares so they could build Fairhope's first wharf for commerce, that's now become the pier, the city's signature recreational attraction.

Now that we have our currency, let's use Aaron Burr's likeness on the money since he passed through Baldwin County. In irons. If you check your history, you'll find buried in the wee small print somewhere that he was found not guilty. The key is to make sure the new nation's dollar holds its value and for that you need a commodity to trade.

My vision, snatched from history, is to build a new wharf, a "green" port to export our goods. What goods? Agriculture, of course, in the tradition of early settlers is our best and already existing prospect. If Texas can have an Organic Cotton Growers Association, then LA or GSA can have a cannabis crop. Yes, there is a long-storied farm history in Baldwin County of growing cotton, soybeans, strawberries, peanuts, pecans, corn, and potatoes. I believe under this new pot plan, there will be again. What crop has extremely high value and can be cultivated on a large scale that has an unlimited market? Marijuana. Forget legalized gambling, that's so Native American. Let's re-envision Jefferson's Agrarian South. Yeah, let's grow thousands of acres of grass. And not just centipede, the heat-tolerant perennial weed called grass. Plush, commercially grown centipede in Baldwin County is resurging. Truckloads of the rolled or rectangular sod are earmarked for farmland turned over for subdivisions and marked for new single-family homes. But now, we could also have the large-scale farmers cultivating Colombian or Acapulco gold. Micro growers could be focused on high quality, high THC strains of Kush, Goo, and Skunk. We'd be competing against our former government for customers. The US Government has been growing pot in Mississippi and has been selling it to people, including Floridian Irv Rosenfeld, since the 1980s. Yes, the 1980s. Here in Alabama, we could get two crops in each year too, I'd bet, but I don't have to bet because we've got farmers, and after a little studying they'll know exactly what Mother Earth can yield. Maybe the Auburn University Cooperative Extension off County Road 104 could help us out. People would look at our crop and think we're nuts, so we'd have to continue to grow some pecans and peanuts.

The local food initiative would supply our community with food. We've got lots of loca-vores already. Heck, the Master Gardeners that frequent the Fairhope Library easily outnumber the librarians. Hippie types who not only live green, they look green. Grass stains, dirt under the nails, a few sticks and twigs in their hair. Their community gardens at Homestead Village and off St. James Avenue are thriving and could become models for expansion.

Simply reducing the layers of government and its regulations means more and better local control. We decide— not some Washington pencil pushers. These are the same bureaucrats who conducted a study on the population of "walruses" and "sea lions." In the Gulf of Mexico! Our own studies, I assure you, will include manatees and dolphins. Our crop needs to be out of the grow houses and back outdoors. In Alabama, we already have the "Sunshine Law," which shines a light on government activity to make sure our state leaders are acting on the up and up. The GSA Sunshine Law will shine Mother Nature's light on our buds.

Let's consider national security. Our former police chief hailed from Miami, a city of, like, 10 million people. I'm confident he can protect LA and even GSA. With everyone so happy with our national crop, I hardly see a need for a defense budget. I like the sound of local militia. It has a revolutionary ring to it and it's grounded in community. Moms, I'm sure, would be glad to keep their sons and daughters on their own nation's soil. Well, perhaps the Mexican drug cartels would have a beef, but most of these criminal gangs are growing marijuana crops in the US. They're already using national parklands and forests.

So, that's the way I see it. At least think about joining my secession movement. But don't take too long, or I'll have to take my leg off and start beating some sense into y'all.

7. Music, Movies, and TV

Q. "Tommy played piano like a kid out in the rain
Then he lost his leg in Dallas he was dancing with the train."

A movie still of "the SPAM scene," approximately an hour into the movie
USS Indianapolis: Men of Courage, starring Nicholas Cage and a few
seconds of me during filming on my day off from the library.

On the Corner of Fourth and York Outside the Louisville Free Public Library

Lincoln, two of me tall, is bronze
Except the tops of his shoes have been
buff-rubbed gold by luck seekers.
His arms cradle burnt red, pale yellow leaves
The trees, naturally, and the manmade Lincoln, majestic

Two sentinels stand on either side of Abraham Lincoln
With fiery orange leaves soaking wet from last night's
rain.
Their crowns are naked, branch veins have blackened
In the trunks of the trees, inverted octopus legs stretching
for sky
Ivy, jealous-green, crawls around the ground and creeps
up the base of the trunk

The prosthetic leg I walk on is carbon fiber, titanium and
acrylic
It's my walking aid.
When I remove it in private, it's my tree stump
Then I am stilled, like the trees.
Most of me lies buried, but my human roots
Run deep beneath the visible scars and boniness.

Legs and Bones

Have you seen *Bones Brigade: An Autobiography*? Well, if you've ever skateboarded, marveled at skateboarders' abilities in a video, or want to see poetry in motion, watch this documentary.

The 2012 film is about the 1980s skateboarding team, Bones Brigade, which was started by Stacy Peralta and George Powell. This film is emotionally and physically powerful. The riders tell their stories and we watch footage showing how they went from the vertical verve of swimming pools to the big air of ramps and how freestyle evolved into street. We see Tony Hawk as a gangly and well-padded teenager riding, sliding, and grinding in an empty pool while Rodney Mullen shows off his mastery of freestyle, riding not just wheels down, but using every side of the board for his tricks. Watching footage of Tony Hawk, I realized that we might have been in the same grade if we went to school together.

I made a diamond-plated steel deck skateboard in my fifth-grade metal shop at Nauset Regional Middle School in Orleans, Massachusetts. Using the band saw, with the teacher standing beside me, I cut out the deck of my new skateboard. It had a surfboard shape, pointy at the nose, and a chopped rear end. I hit the toggle power switch on the grinder and it whirred to life. I pushed the board into the spinning disk and it sounded like a machine gun, tat a tat tat a tat tat a tat, and the sparks came flying off that thing like sparklers on the Fourth of July. I rested my board on the table in front of the grinder and pushed it gently at first into the spinning wheels. Ggggrrrrr. Crap! I just gouged a groove in the rail, forgetting that you have to move the deck side to side. I remember putting the deck in a large vice, and I bent the kicktail to my liking. It was a big deal when the wheels finally came in. We had been staring at the trucks for what seemed like months. In fact, I think I made a lamp while we waited for the wheels to arrive. Those polyurethane wheels were gold! No, more like rays of sunshine because you could see into them, like a kaleidoscope. They were clear. That summer my sister Lynne and I practically rode the wheels off that board, but I remember one night the best. We had fireflies and firecrackers, like every summer. I can still see those kicktail flames lighting up the end of my summer night run down the driveway into Nanumet Drive.

In their video *Animal Chin*, these kids are on the road sharing a hotel room and sleeping with their boards. It reminded me of Hendrix lying horizontal with his guitar, or Gretzky sleeping with his hockey stick, or me with my journal open on my chest, asleep, still gripping a pen. Most people who are passionate about something seem to have spent some time sleeping with their objects of affection.

"The objects we grow up with help form our sense of the world," Elizabeth Kostova writes in the current *Poets & Writers* magazine article "No Ideas but in Things: The Importance of First Objects." This is true not only for athletes, and musicians, and writers, but for amputees too. For leg amputees, I'd go a step further and say, our prosthesis forms our sense of self because we have limited mobility without a prosthesis. That said, I can count the number of times I actually slept with my leg on. It's probably less than my ten fingers and five toes.

Many of the men interviewed from the team weep openly at the memory of the time they spent in the Bones Brigade. With his head leaning to the side, Lance Mountain sheds a tear at the power of the relationships, the memories, and the experience in the Bones Brigade, a team he never felt worthy of being a part of, now or then. Rodney Mullen and Tony Hawk were called "freaks" not by their families or their teammates, but by other skateboarders. In part, they were doing things their peers didn't understand. They weren't just skating, they were creating and innovating. In the documentary, Mullen said we "create through controlled desperation."

I miss my circa 1978 skateboard. It sat, mostly unused, in the cellar for 20 years. Every once in a while, I'd hop on it, always goofy-footed, and tip back the tail, or do a 180 while looking out for the lally column to make sure if I fell I wouldn't crack my skull open on the way to the cement floor. When we moved to Alabama, I donated it to the swap shop at the dump. I hope some kid got a few kicks, or learned a few tricks, before she cut her ankle on the unforgiving steel rails.

In the film, Rodney Mullen talked about the community he had as part of the skateboarding team and how it had its own vocabulary, expression, and motion. He talks today about the importance of community, but I think they had more than community; it was a culture. Writers, Kostova says, "don't outgrow the realm of childhood observation; in a way, we stay stuck in a sense of the vividness of things." It is this vividness of prosthetics and the character of amputees, both in life and literature, that I've been exploring and writing about for years. Kostova reminds writers that "the first objects we really study in life teach us not only to see but to look." Looking at Hawk, Mountain, and Mullen as individuals connected to the skateboarding scene, I see how my prosthesis connects me to an amputee culture. I call us The Leg Bones Brigade.

Movie Extra Audition: How Did It Go?

"I was told an hour ago that 44 extras were coming to audition for five parts." Suzanne Massingill of Barefoot Models and Talent tells the 35 guys in the room, most of them standing.

A small white board on the wall read:

USS INDY SAG-AFTRA Auditions

Shoot Date Starts June 19

Have your Head Shot

Hearing a song playing softly in the background, I felt the "Radioactive" testosterone in the room. Hell, I was radioactive. Nervous. Excited. Explosive! Despite all the stress, I could have proudly worn my nephew Zach's "I pooped today" T-shirt. We were all, well, they were all a handsome, well-groomed group of guys, but we were cramped in our own flatulence-filled, higgledy-piggledy office scene bubble. Even the military guys, both active and retired, were tense. So tense, one guy said, to no one in particular and everyone who arrived after him, "If you're on time, you're late."

All the tension was an indication of how badly we wanted to be a part of the first big-screen movie to honor the men and the memories of those who served on the *USS Indianapolis*.

Shut the front door! That's what I would have told you if I didn't see Hannibal Pictures producer Richard Rionda Del Castro and director Mario Van Peebles walk in through the same door I did. Van Peebles, a little shorter than I expected, was the Lenny Kravitz of *LA Law,* or was he the Ice-T of *Law and Order*? I've seen him and that captivating smile on a couple of episodes of *Nashville*.

The producer came out of the room, not to make a curtain call, but to welcome us. He said, "I've been trying to make this picture for 10 years." He went back through the door, or as I like to call it, the portal to Hollywood fame.

Suzanne called the first name on the list.

"He left," someone said. Great, I thought, one less person to contend with.

The casting agency put out a call specifically for amputee extras. I looked around for other leg amputees to size up my competition I saw five guys wearing shorts. Limbs intact. I watched how people were walking around the room. No amputee I've ever met walks perfectly, not yet anyway. There's usually a hitch, a leg whip, or a limp, but so far nothing. The glint of my carbon fiber and titanium catches the eyes of Suzanne, several hopeful extras, and most importantly, the producer.

The guy to my left was called and came out smiling after being in the room less than thirty seconds.

The guy to my right was in there for like an hour, but it was really just minutes. After a couple of muffled rounds of laughter he sat back down next to me with two pages from the "shooting script."

Audition: (more than 15 seconds but less than 120)

It happened so fast I couldn't even describe the room I walked into. I only wanted to answer their questions without puking or farting from my mind's gastrointestinal excitement.

I walk in and shake the hands of four people including "Rick" and "Mario." The producer asked questions like Rambo going all M-60 on Hope, Washington.

Producer: How old are you?

Alan: 47, but no military experience, I'm a born amputee. (Cool! I wanted to work that in.)

Producer: That's alright; can you swim?

Alan: Lifelong swimmer, taught by a lifeguard (true story).

Producer: We'll be shooting lots of scenes in a large water tank; any problems with prolonged periods of time in standing water? (My *Dances with Wolves* name is Stands without a Leg...in Water.)

Alan: No, I'm a floater too. (Did I really just say that? Yep, me and the Baby Ruth in *Caddyshack*.)

Producer: Any problems being in the water with actors around you?

Alan: No. (Really? Is this a question someone wanting a part as an extra would say yes to?)

Mario: (pointing at my prosthesis) How far down does your real leg go? (Stump The Librarian knows this one.)

Alan: About six inches below the knee.

Producer: Okay, we'll be shooting with actors behind you, in the tank.

Alan: I know the story, I read *In Harm's Way*. (I didn't have time to say I was a librarian or that I never would have known about this story or been so fascinated by history without the movie *Jaws*.)

Producer: (to assistant) Take a headshot.

Mario: (to iPhone-holding assistant) Get his leg! (You had me at hello, Mario.)

Producer: Em, yeah, a full body shot.

Mario: Thanks for coming in.

Alan: (with a half-smile to Mario) Thanks for the opportunity.

Alan: (eye contact with producer) I really hope to hear back from you. (No one will cooperate more fully with the animatronic sharks than me.)

Producer: (eye to eye with me) You will.

On Set with an Amputee

R.1. "And this was my Hollywood career."

Day I

I show up under the Perdido Pass Bridge in Orange Beach, Alabama, at 11 AM carrying my belongings, including a towel, cell phone, wallet, keys (in a Ziploc bag), and a copy of *On the Road*, in a blue Otto Bock sling bag. The parking area under the bridge is full of trucks and trailers.

A man at wardrobe walks through an open sliding glass door, out of an air-conditioned truck, and steps down onto a platform that rises up and down like a beer delivery truck. Patrick gives me a pair of blue denim sailor pants, a white T-shirt, and a long sleeve blue denim shirt.

"You can change in the trailer marked BG," he says. I walk down the row and see BG handwritten on a strip of masking tape stuck to the door. Later in the day, I learn BG stands for Back Ground. I grab the handrail to climb up the three steps into what was really a bunk room with an adjacent toilet and sink.

I change quickly and head back to the wardrobe truck, where they cut my right pant leg, make some jagged cuts, and add some fake blood to the denim.

I meet Paul, a production assistant, and we walk past Cobalt restaurant and over to the docks where boats are ferrying everyone to the set, a rig in the Gulf of Mexico just south and west of the Flora-Bama.

On Location

Stacy, the makeup artist, and I take a boat ride with Alan, the boat owner and ferry service provider, to the set. It's my first time on the water in the Gulf of Mexico. I've been fishing, sightseeing, and whale watching in the Atlantic and whale watching in the Pacific on a Zodiac off the Oregon coast and highly recommend the experiences. It feels satisfying to finally complete the trinity of boating on and swimming in the three major North American seas.

I step onto the dock floating alongside the rig. The first thing I notice is the pile of bodies wearing the same get-up I have on.

Stacy heads to the galley, which is air-conditioned.

"I apologize in advance for the smell," I tell the women around me, and Zach, the arm amputee. "It's the Gulf Coast in the summer."

"Oh, don't worry about it," Stacy says, and so I pretend not to worry and doff the leg and lean it against a cabinet.

Stacy begins dabbing and glomping red and black goo on my stump with a wooden tongue depressor.

The silicone is red, black, and textured to the point that Stacy "builds it up" really well. So well, in fact, it's heavy and I begin wondering what ill effects it will have once I get it all off and put the prosthesis back over the stump. When I see my residual limb it's red and raw. It looks like it's on fire.

At the same time Stacy is applying gruesomeness, four other hands are on me.

Melody, a blue-eyed and blue-green-haired makeup artist from LA (Los Angeles not Lower Alabama), applies sunburn. Amber, Stacy's auburn-haired business partner, runs her greased-up fingers through my hair. She tells me it's a concoction of charcoal powder and castor oil.

"Oh, so it's all natural?" I ask.

"Yeah," Amber says, and Melody just giggles.

"Everyone outta here, we have to set up for lunch," John, the bearded caterer, tells everyone in the galley.

"Not without help," I say to everyone within earshot of me. I'm suddenly, and quite uncomfortably, now dependent on others for mobility.

Extra Bobby and Extra John step inside the galley to help me.

On Set

They set me down in Video Village, an area where extras are not allowed. Video Village is at the front of the rig and facing south to the Gulf, right behind the camera and where all the playback screens and monitors are located. It's also protected from the elements by an Easy Up, and for makeup touch ups.

"Good timing," the director's daughter tells me with a smile, and she gets in line for lunch.

Amber brings me a lunch of steak tips, rice, and broccoli. Melody makes a special trip and brings me back dessert: red velvet upside down cake with white chocolate chips and cream cheese frosting.

At lunch, all the fashion-conscious women are impressed by Zach and me, the amputee extras. We recommend Hobo purses and wallets, a brand none of them had heard of before, but one both our significant others swear by.

After lunch is a costume change: get out of pants, take off denim shirt.

A woman with a wiffle haircut, asks/tells me to put on two pairs of boxers, as just one is see through once it gets wet. Lillian is the skinniest person on the rig and, as you'll see, we become close. She helps me get to the laundry room, which is next to the galley. Up the steps, through the hatch door, I notice the tattoo on her forearm.

"It's a mathematical symbol," Lillian says, but I'm thinking it's more geometric. It looks a lot like the Deathly Hallows symbol from the Harry Potter books and movies.

And speaking of books, I see a copy of *Only 317 Survived!*, which is one of the books the movie is based on.

Lillian, who had just been talking about pizza porn on Tumblr during lunch, holds a towel up across the door to block passersby from seeing me bare-assed. We exchange awkward pleasantries, and I really have no idea if she's even still holding the towel because it takes all my concentration to stand on one leg, take off denim pants, and my Hanes and then slip on two pairs of boxers that are two sizes too big. With lightning speed, Lillian is standing next to me, pinching the boxers in the back, has a needle and thread in her hands, and is tailoring them to fit me.

"That should hold," she says. She's smiling confidently. Wardrobe humor? Not funny. I'm the kind of guy who doesn't like to go out without a prosthesis on and here I am in my skivvies with a couple hundred people around.

When I"m back in my chair, Lillian is by my side tying a strip of denim around my right thigh.

Rehearsal

Saunders, a man of color with freckles and an Einstein Afro, comes by and says, "Mario (Van Peebles) wants to talk about the scene you are in; can you come with me?"

"I need a little help."

"Oh! Yeah! Here, which side is better?" Saunders says, as I raise my right arm and he dips his left shoulder under my arm and props me up. I grab onto anything I can get my hand on to hop as little as possible, and I hop, shuffle, and slide toward the front of the set, near the director's area that has a camera and other equipment under a black hood.

Mario sets the scene for us and we are going to rehearse it. With my right hand I hold onto the left shoulder of the man with the megaphone.

"First, everyone just introduce yourself."

"Nic (Cage), Joey, Alan, Marley, Tom (Sizemore), Jarrod."

"You've been on a raft for two days," Mario sets the scene. Captain McVeigh, played by Nic, passes around some SPAM, which we all fake taking a bite of and pass along.

"That's great," Mario says. Now we are passing along a canteen's cap full of water that everyone must get one small sip from. So we pass it around and take our fake sips.

After our run-through, I say, "Ah, Mario, they just changed my wardrobe and need to add more to my stump."

He's staring at it, and sees there is not enough blood below the tourniquet.

"Ok, Saunders help...what's your name?"

"Alan."

"Help Alan out."

The cool thing is that Saunders already knows my name. He, along with another guy, help me to the nearest seat.

I sit in an "Actor" chair one away from Nic, who is drinking an Aquafina water, while Stacy adds more blood and hanging flesh to my stump. I look over and give him the head bob; he smiles and says, "Getting some work done I see."

"Yeah, it's getting nastier looking."

He nods and walks a few feet away while Stacy applies more makeup. By this time, everybody on the rig, and I mean everybody, is waiting for me to shoot the next scene. But as my friend Rivers wrote in a recent email, "Alan, that leg takes you places." And sure enough, I find myself checking off another item on the extras list of Don'ts. Do not sit in "Actors' chairs," which ironically enough are actually directors' chairs.

After Saunders and one other person grab onto me, the props guy drops some dog tags over my head, and says "tuck them into your T-shirt." The guys get me to and over the rig railing, and down the ladder into "John Rambo's" Zodiac boat. I sit next to Nic, but don't say anything to him. He's rehearsing lines.

Shooting a Scene in Gulf Waters

It's a twenty-yard boat ride, a distance I could swim faster than the boat travels. Mario, using a microphone to amplify his voice above the sea, gives all of us directions about where he wants us in the life rafts.

"Camera's up."

"You, you," Mario's pointing at me.

"What's your name again?"

"Alan."

"Move left, right, move your leg, put it on the side of the raft." If he tells me to "do the hokey pokey and shake it all about," I will take his direction.

"Rolling," the guy holding the bullhorn says.

Mario disappears under the hood.

"Action!"

In one of the takes, the extra who's supposed to be feeding me, is vomiting. So I improvise by shifting and lifting myself while gritting and wrenching to get the rations from the other guy. It turns out Extra Jarrod gets seasick because he didn't take enough Dramamine. If I'm only visible in one scene, this will probably be it. Here's me: stump in the air, sipping water and a guy barfing in my background. In fact, many of the crew didn't survive because they drank seawater, and vomiting is one of the first side effects.

I lose track of the number of takes we shoot, and the number of SPAM bites we actually eat.

On the Rig

Back over the rail and onto the rig, with a little help from an extra friend and a man named Tommy, who lives in Fairhope.

I sit down on a folding chair, and Lillian whisks over and hands me a towel.

Mario walks over.

"Nice job!" We fist bump.

"Thanks," I say, "glad to be a part of this."

"That's a wrap for you!"

Stacy applies some clear solution to help me get the silicone off the leg.

She tries helping but it is touchy with my hair sticking to the silicone. It feels nice when it goes on, but it stings quite a bit when you have to remove it.

"I don't want to hurt you," Stacy says.

"I don't want you to either," I say, and she laughs. I use the tourniquet to brush, scrape, pull, and peel the silicone off my stump.

Lillian and I get off on the wrong foot. She is in wardrobe and after I am out of makeup, I tell her that the tourniquet fell off in the water. Actually, the torn shirt I was using as instructed by McVeigh to keep my head wet, was swallowed up by the Gulf sometime between takes. "I don't believe you," is the look she gives me.

Under the Bridge

Back at "Base Camp" I change out of my wardrobe and fill out paperwork for Sam so I can get paid $125 for the day.

The people on set treat me like a star, not an extra.

Being superstitious, I keep the tourniquet hoping it will help me get a callback the next day.

Double Take

R.2. "I suddenly began to realize that everybody in America is a natural-born thief. I was getting the bug myself."

Day Two

I arrive at Base Camp at 9:20 AM and see Paul, Jarrod, Zach, and Saunders milling around wardrobe. My outfit, which I had taken off on the rig, has magically appeared on the mainland. I change into my boxers and T-shirt in the BG trailer.

I see the guy from Fairhope again. He grabs a water out of the cooler and I notice the back of his shirt. It says "Ship-Faced."

"I love that shirt," I tell him, "what'syournameagain?"

"It's Tommy and thanks." I notice it has OBA, the acronym for Orange Beach, on the front pocket.

I find out that Tommy is a grip and we hit it off so well that I tell him my wife, Susan, and I bought a lot in Fairhope and will be building a new house soon.

"Hey, congratulations, that's exciting news," he says.

"Yeah! It is, and thanks, check it out if you can."

Actor Joey (playing Alvin) steps down out of his trailer.

"They are filming Day 4 raft scenes today, and I'm doing my stunt later."

"That's awesome!" I say, happy for that nugget of information about our scene together. He tells me about the fight scene and how he falls "like 25 feet."

"I'm going back in my trailer to eat my breakfast burrito."

"Okay, later."

Very little waiting yesterday, but we are making up for it today. It's already been two hours, and I'm still here at Base Camp.

All of a sudden, it's go time and people are running around like they just stepped on a fire ant mound.

Paul, the production assistant, has two walkie talkies and two cell phones. He seems to manage them all rather nicely, and still talk to me, the person standing next to him, while we wait at the marina. Minutes later, we are joined on the dock by amputee extra Zach and Stacy, who reminds me of my sister Laurie.

On Set

There are none cooler under pressure than makeup and wardrobe. I call them out because they are the people responsible for transforming me from a fake leg-wearing amputee into a humble, skivvies-wearing sailor whose stump has been shredded into something completely foreign, even to its owner. Stacy, the silicone wonder worker, Amber my oiler and Dawn patrol guru, and Melody my sunburner and eye blackener all work together to bring me, and many other extras, as director Mario says, "near death."

Prop man comes by and tries dropping a set of dog tags over my head again. The opening is much smaller, and I have to pull and wiggle them over my head.

Lillian is tying a tourniquet around my thigh.

"Mmmmmm," she says, looking at a picture of me on her phone from the day before. "This one's shorter." She walks away and then quickly comes back with my denim rag prop.

Today is Day 4 in the rafts and we act on the direction that we spot a plane, then see a plane dropping supplies, and finally watch the seaplane in the air that will later land and rescue us. FYI: There are no planes we can see flying, but there would be if we ask Siri to find "planes overhead."

In the Water

Our group is down from ten people and three rafts to five people and two rafts.

I'm in the same raft with Joey, Nic, and Marley but I'm schlumped over the opposite side of the life raft with my back to the two guys who have lines. Jarrod is solo in the smaller raft.

There is time between takes. The extras are silent as Nic and Alvin talk about acting, makeup, movies, etc. Alvin recommends a book called *Wanderer* (by Sterling Hayden) and Nic says he's interested in it. I want to say "I'm a librarian, and I'm interested in that book too," but because of my status as an extra and physical position in the raft facing away from them, I keep quiet.

I relax between takes, and though I'm mostly in the water I lean my back against the side of the raft and look over at my raft mates, Joey, Nic, and Marley, the director's son; who is sitting beside me. I'm not the kind to get starstruck, Nic's just another guy in the boat who gets the lines and the most camera face time. Plus Mario is a great motivator, very supportive, and always positive with the actors and extras. Mario's ability to empathize with actors makes him an actors' director. Between takes there is a lot of talk about "close-ups," "wide angles," and "camera speed."

The Zodiac comes by several times with Nic's makeup person. She is touching him up during the time between takes.

Mario on the bullhorn: "Thanks for your patience, guys. We're changing the camera battery."

I notice a pattern on the water's surface a few yards away indicating a school of fish. Does anyone else notice the fish swimming all around the rafts?

With all these fish swimming around us, I wonder if we are being served up to the Gulf Coast sharks as lunch. Later on, one of the special effects guys says the rig is surrounded by an electromagnetic pulse, kind of like an electronic fence that keeps your dog in the yard. The sharks don't like the pulse so they stay away, in theory.

I point as an osprey pulls a fish out of the sea, gripping it within his talons.

"Check it out." Just as I say it, the fish falls back to the sea. As Alvin and Nic look over, Nic says, "What kind of bird is that?"

"It's an osprey," I say. "Some people call them sea hawks."

We watch the bird fly north, toward shore, and out of sight.

"There are bald eagles around here too," I blurt out.

"At the beach?" Nic asks. Is he trying to Stump the Librarian?

"Not sure about here, but definitely in Mobile Bay, and all across the Delta," I say.

"I didn't know that. I thought they were only in the northwest, like Alaska," Nic adds.

"Well, I think they've made a resurgence here and all around the country."

Marley pushes me on the right shoulder and points up above the rig. All eyes look up to see the osprey land on the top of the crane, settle his wings, and start scanning the Gulf looking for his next catch.

We shoot two scenes, with everyone "near death." For every take, I'm facing away from my raft mates, stump resting on the side, and right arm and shoulder draped over the side of the raft.

Nic and Joey are talking about what to do this weekend. They are staying in Mobile.

"You should visit my hometown, Fairhope, across the bay," I tell them. They stare at me, like they've never heard of it.

"It's a nice walkable downtown and it's great for families too," I add, sounding like the Chamber of Commerce.

"Picture's up," I hear. I say to myself, "Saved by the megaphone."

"Rolling, rolling." I settle into my sideways position and instead of tensing up, I relax, rest my head on my blue denim rag, and feel the sea roll beneath me. I close my eyes just as the camera enters my peripheral vision, and remember the method to this madness is "near death."

"Action!"

On the Rig

Mario comes by after conferring with Saunders, points at me and says, "You're wrapped."

"Am I gonna' live?" I ask.

"Are you gonna' live?" Mario smiles and then starts laughing. "That's funny." Now I'm smiling. Everyone around is all EF Hutton, listening. People on the rig resort to observation, eavesdropping, snooping, and general skullduggery to find out WTF is going on. It turns out nobody knows WTF is going on, so I continue to press the only one who actually knows what's going on, Mario.

"Seriously, I'm not being philosophical, I'm being literal. I want to know if my character dies."

"You're still here, aren't you?" Mario says, and keeps on walking, but I still don't have an answer.

He and Saunders speak privately a few feet away. Saunders comes over and says, "You should get a callback for Monday."

True Story

While I'm sitting in Video Village next to Bama, a main character, who is getting make-upped, producer Richard Rionda Del Castro introduces us to a woman who is the grandchild of a USS Indianapolis survivor. I learn later from a Channel 5 interview that Bama's late grandfather was also a survivor. The granddaughter turns her phone toward us and flicks through pictures of her granddad, in uniform, on board the ship, and posing in Hawaii with a hula girl. Just as I notice how tall he looks, she says, "He was six feet, five inches." She mentions, in a lighter moment, the Navy being known for its low narrow doorways, and how he always had to "duck."

She gives Bama, Richard, and myself a personal detail of what helped him survive in the water.

"He held a potato in his hand the whole time." I look down at my own hand, imagine a potato. "That's all he had to hold onto."

Grateful to hear such a personal and moving story, I think to myself, "Alan, the leg not only takes you places, it puts you in the right place too." I thank her for sharing the details and the photos with us, and Bama says, "We just want this movie to honor the men and tell their story."

Back to Base Camp

On the boat ride back, Melody and I sit next to each other on the bench in front of the captain. A rogue wave hits the bow of Tony's boat sending a wall of water at us just seconds after I put Melody's phone in my plastic Ziploc baggie. Having a cell phone on set is another item on the extras don't list. As an amputee, it's another thing I can actually do, or, at least get away with. Yesterday, I took a picture of my stump under the table, so I have a record of Stacy's fantastic work.

Dog Tags

Taking off my wardrobe, I grab for the dog tags and notice the name. E. B. Sledge. Of all the dog tags in the props department, I get the pair that belongs to a man whose son still lives in Fairhope. Up until a few years ago, John Sledge wrote a book column for the *Mobile Press-Register* that avid readers, librarians, and lovers of literature read religiously. I've only met John a few times, but he's a well-known and much respected author in Lower Alabama. Anyway, his father's memoir, *With the Old Breed: At Peliliu and Okinawa,* is the basis for the HBO series *The Pacific*, and probably the reason the props department for this film has a set of his dog tags. The actor who played him in that series, Joseph Mazzello, probably wore these very same dog tags. When I saw the name, I suddenly felt humbled and very proud at the same time. Humbled by the actions and respectful of his writings and of all the World War II service men and women.

Trailer

I walk into a trailer to do paperwork so I can get paid, and who do I meet? Cam, the screenplay writer. It sounds unbelievable, but it's true. It doesn't hurt that I'll talk to just about anybody. I guess that's the journalist in me. I'm curious about people, and want to find out their stories. These traits serve me pretty well at Fairhope Public Library too. I tell Cam I'm an essayist and blogger with an MFA from Spalding University. He talks about writing and character and how the screenplay for the film was developed, using several sources including *In Harm's Way*. He explains that the story is "inspired by" true events and many of the secondary characters are composites from actions and experiences of survivors. Cam reminds me a bit of Woody Allen, with his rectangular framed lenses and his fine wavy hair. As he's leaning forward to read his green copy of the shooting script, I notice he's constantly sweeping the hair away from his eyes and face.

"So you're the script writer and the script doctor?" I ask, as I notice him making notations on the script in his hands.

"Yeah. I'm working on adding a scene that we had removed back into the script."

He asks, "Are you an actor?"

"No, I'm an amputee," I say, and I laugh at that since it's obvious. "When they did a call for amputees I auditioned as an extra with Mario and Tim, one of the producers." Cam asks about my impression of it all.

"Oh, it's been a great experience and a great opportunity to check off the bucket list. "I want to thank Mario for using actual amputees in his movie, instead of just green screening everything."

"Mario's awesome and it was 100 percent his idea to use actual amputees to film some scenes."

"It was great talking to you, Cam."

"You too, Alan."

On the Road

On the drive home, I feel physically and mentally exhausted. After a ten-hour day, an hour and a half in the water, we probably shot less than two minutes of film that will be in the final cut of the movie. My mind starts to wander, drift really, so I pull over for a minute and close my eyes. I see the osprey, so majestic and strong, dropping his catch again. I begin to wonder if the osprey is becoming my albatross.

Wrapped

R.3. "Everyone looked like a broke-down movie extra."

Day Three

I arrive on Monday in time for a full breakfast of pancakes, eggs, grits, bacon, fruit, yogurt, orange juice, and coffee, courtesy of Sessions Productions.

I see Tommy while I'm eating. We talk about our weekends.

"I rode my bike down your street over the weekend," he says.

"Did you check out the lot we are building on? It's the one with the big live oaks in the front."

"Is it next to a house going up?"

"Yeah, it is."

"It's a nice piece of land and those trees are beautiful."

"Thanks. Stop and say 'hey' if you see me on the lot while it's being built."

"I'll do that," he says.

Read

I have time to socialize and find out how Friday night at the Flora-Bama Yacht Club went. Extra Bobby says it was a great time and the party didn't end until 3 AM.

I'm still waiting around Base Camp at 10:30 AM so I open *On the Road* and start reading.

Ride

Finally they call the extras. Several of us, including Extra Bobby, a retired Navy Veteran with two tours in Iraq and one in Afghanistan, and the special effects people take the boat ride to the rig. We hear from big hat and big beard effects guy that the plane is on set today and we are shooting the rescue.

"After that," he says, "we're moving locations to film at night."

The day hasn't even started and he speaks from experience as he says, "Shooting at two locations is a lot for one day."

I don't go directly to makeup on the rig today. I hang out with the extras on the back of the platform, and we battle one another for a place to sit. We get our face, hands, and necks made up in the back of the rig shadows. Prop man hands us all our dog tags.

"Thanks, you gave me Sledge's, the same ones I had Friday." He looks at me, confused.

"That doesn't happen very often."

"It's a good sign," I say, as he hands a set to extra Barrett. He's a professional disc golfer I met while introducing some people to the sport at the course in Fairhope. It was great to see a familiar face and we pass the time chatting. He knows Tommy too because they play disc golf together.

"Man," one extra says, "It's 12:30 and we haven't even gotten wet yet."

There's a buzz as Nic arrives on set.

Sam calls me up to Video Village. I say hello to all the makeup and wardrobe women who are busy with actors, not extras.

The rig is unusually full today. Everyone involved with the production is on set and there are lots more chairs set up for the movie's producers under the Video Village tent.

One producer is barking at everyone to "pray for the sun." Everyone ignores him.

"The PBY is in the air," Mario announces with the bullhorn about the incoming seaplane.

A few minutes later he walks by Marley and me, more excited and animated than his son and says, "You're being rescued today!"

"Awesome, Mario!" I shout, and a few guys yell, but it sounds lame because no one is in sync.

"ETA 10 minutes."

It should be arriving from the north any minute now. It comes into sight over my right shoulder and is cruising fairly low. It looks like a boat with wings.

As impressive as the sight of it is, the sound is even better. The steady Bwaaa bw bwaaa is mean and powerful, and a little worrisome, like it's not firing on all cylinders. Everyone is standing, craning their necks to get a good long look at the seaplane. It makes a second pass for the camera. It circles again and lands rather roughly. It has a massive wake as much of the plane seems to be below the water line.

An hour passes, and Nic comes out of the galley, his makeshift trailer, and says, "I'll see you for the night shoot."

Everybody is looking at each other, wondering what's happening. It takes another half hour to reach me that the plane broke down and that there will be no plane rescue scene.

"Rolling."

They are shooting underwater scenes with the sharks circling and attacking the rafts.

"Cut."

Shark

The animatronic shark is swinging over our heads from a crane. I grab my iPhone. Just as I'm ready to tap, I hear, "No pictures, Alan." Sam, the PA, is in the right spot at the wrong time. I listen this time. It's a tiger shark, and it looks very real, glistening in the sun, yet still seawater slick.

The animatronic shark goes into its own suitcase. It's wrapped!

At 3 PM, Tiffany removes my leg makeup.

"That's 30 minutes." We break for lunch. Lasagna, salad, collard greens, watermelon, and lemon bars for dessert.

"This location is a wrap."

Still in our movie wardrobes, we wait for the boats to take us to Base Camp while they move the whole production from the rig to a barge on the Intracoastal Waterway, about six nautical miles away.

We arrive at the Base Camp location, which is practically empty, like a carnival that has up and disappeared. All that remains is one trailer and a wardrobe truck.

Under the bridge, I pour Skittles directly into my mouth like a confectionary troll. We wait for someone to call our name, give us some news, tell us where to be, or what to do. Your life as an extra is to follow instructions. The only problem is we receive very few instructions. It's been a hurry up and wait day. There are 20 extras today and nobody, including my eastern European friend and Gulf Shores resident, "have been in the water."

We are told the new base camp is off Canal Road, not far from the breakfasts and Bloody Marys of Brick and Spoon.

We have two hours before we are due at the new base camp. I have an extra take a picture of me.

Cool Treat

I drive to Dairy Queen. I walk in and order a Reese's Blizzard. I wait for it, and a family of four waits beside me. The little girl is staring at me. I'm used to being stared at. Does she think the amputation is recent? There have been shark sightings along the Gulf, including hammerheads.

189

"I'm in a movie," I tell the girl with braids like Pippi Longstocking. Her expression doesn't change. I know thanks to makeup my face looks fried and blistered, but Pippi's dad looks like he's burnt crispier than I am. His sunburn is going to hurt for a while. Mine will wash off, sometime today.

"Reese's Blizzard," someone says, and I move up to the counter to see she's already inserted the spoon. She flips the cup upside down. I should put some of this on that guy's face. Naw, that's wasting it, and I think how foolish I would be to expect a third meal as part of my extra benefits.

Cut

When I get to the new Base Camp, I see Tracy chucking a football in a parking area near the trailers.

More people arrive on scene around 8 PM. We are all hungry, and can smell food, but only the actors get to eat.

Another hour goes by and I pass the time chitchatting and reading from the parking lot light.

"It's a wrap for today!" Maggie, the chain-smoking blonde says.

"We're wrapped!" I had spent twelve hours waiting at base camp, in makeup, on set, waiting for the rescue scene to be filmed. It didn't happen. I am weary, upset, angry, and relieved in a span of 12 seconds.

Reflection in the Mirror

For the first and only time, I step up into the makeup trailer. Tom Sizemore is saying thanks to Lauren and exiting the other door. Alvin, my raft mate, is getting the grease rinsed out of his hair. I look around, half tired, when a fresh and familiar voice calls out amidst the confusion and bright light from the bulbs reflecting off the mirrors.

190

"Over here, Alan," Stacey says, and I brighten at a friendly and familiar face.

"Have a seat," she says and I plop down into the barber chair, exhausted from doing nothing, except breathing in the wet, salty, Alabama air, intermixed with the diesel from nearby generators. She uses baby oil and "99" to clean my face, neck, and arms.

The casting agent called me on Thursday. I told her I couldn't make it. I like to think that by not showing up, my character didn't make it. In a movie inspired by real events, even I did not see my character surviving four days at sea. What was keeping the character alive? A denim tourniquet strip.

It doesn't really matter what I think; if they want my character to survive, all they have to do is grab another extra, like Barrett, bloody his knee cap, fly the green screen, and put him in the background. It's Hollywood; by the time they are done editing, the movie-goer will never know the difference.

Oddly enough, the reality is not the movie, it's in the movie-making, and the people who work in front of and behind the cameras. It's not about where the movie is going, it's how it gets there. Just like Sal in *On the Road*.

My chances of actually being background seem better than most simply because I was in the same boat with Nic, Tom, Joey and a few other actors.

The last Nic Cage movie shot in Mobile, *Tokarev*, was renamed *Rage* and went straight to video.

USS Indianapolis: Men of Courage went straight to video too. I attended the showing with my family: Susan, Kim, Steve, Mary, Uncle Bill, Ben, and Alexa, at the Saenger Theatre in Mobile. We screened the movie for my fans, including my brother Mark and Sue's parents John and Helen at the Fairhope Library.

8. Reading Room Patrons

S. "The library was church without the collection plate."

Sue and I with the Olympic Mountain Range
in the background. Olympic National Park, Washington

Warrior Queen Library Patron

I hear it immediately. The unmistakable clink and clank of aluminum crutches echo from the tile and off the walls of the cavernous Colony Room. A woman with brown hair pulled back in a pony tail crutches in and stands at the circulation desk. I can hear her voice, but it's a hushed library voice. After talking with Jane, she heads my way, the reference desk at the Fairhope Public Library. The tinny echo muffles once she crosses the threshold from tile to carpet. I see her above-the-knee stump ends around mid-thigh. The socked residual limb is angling, or listing, 30 degrees from below her shorts. She crutches quickly by my desk toward the children's area.

When she went by, we made eye contact for a split second. It was library quiet when I glimpsed her dark brown eyes. I thought about saying something, but I didn't. I considered showing her my prosthesis, but that seemed ridiculous, not knowing her situation. Seeing her made me feel like I was staring at myself years ago. I didn't like what I saw on her face. The same scowl of pent-up misery and pain I see on her face is a not-so-distant memory. I felt I failed. I did nothing. As a fellow amputee I should have acted. Why? Am I supposed to have some common bond among amputees like we all belong to some one-legged tribe?

Then I thought about Warrior-Queen Vishpla. She is the first and only female amputee I've read about from ancient times. Her story comes from the Rig Veda, one of four sacred Hindu writings from the Vedic era, which occurred between 1500 and 500 B.C. Vishpla, according to the story, loses her leg in battle. She later rejoins the fight wearing an iron prosthesis. It seemed more than coincidental that I'd seen this woman without a prosthesis in the library. After all, I learned about

194

Vishpla, the first written record of a person wearing a prosthesis, in a library book. I like to believe Vishpla, upon returning to the battlefield, was hailed with chants of "Warrior Queen! Warrior Queen!"

In my mind, I put that iron leg on my crutching patron and watched her walk through the library. Crutch free now! Vishpla wasn't wielding a sword, swinging for heads, or slashing torsos on the battlefield anymore. Head high, shoulders back, the Warrior Queen Patron strode unsteadily to my desk and gave me a nod and a smile. As she walked past me she carried something that for me is much more powerful than a sword: books.

Rumpled Stump Skin

Paul came into the library yesterday, on crutches. As a fast walker, I nearly ran into him when he was coming out of periodicals to look at the new books.

He was wearing shorts. His stump, like all stumps, dangles as if defying gravity, knee is flexed, if slightly. It's an odd observation, and I mention it because my stump does the same thing. It is not rigid, it kind of hangs there, looking sort of useless, like a penguin's flipper when he's on land.

Paul's residual limb wasn't exposed because he was wearing a stump shrinker. Once you remove your leg from the routine of being in a steel trap for 15-20 hours a day, it has a way of rebelling by swelling and turning shades of red, crimson, and then purple leaning toward blue, as in "Violet you're turning violet."

"I've got an open wound and can't put my leg on," Paul said. I know open wounds or sores on your stump means your $15,000 prosthesis is probably going to be "for display only" in your house until you heal. Knowing that it was not so much the pain as it was the inability to wear a leg, I asked, "Have you seen Jeff?" We've been going to the same prosthetist, and that's where we first met. He had, but Jeff didn't offer any advice, except to leave the leg off.

"I hate these things." He must have said it a half dozen times during our conversation in the middle of the Fairhope Public Library. It wasn't the open wound he hated, or his prosthesis, but the abysmal consequences of using crutches for mobility. This is the same guy who doesn't think twice about popping his leg off in the library, sometimes at the drop of a hat. It reminds me of the way some people want to pour out all their problems to me, the reference desk bartender. Or maybe it's like reference radar, the feeling I get when I know someone is waiting at the desk without having to actually see a patron. Call it a sixth sense, but don't confuse it with six degrees from Kevin Bacon (I'm three degrees from Hollywood's everyman).

Crutches make you ashamed of your body, and embarrassed by your appearance. I've been fortunate, I only use my wooden crutches in the house. I can speak from past experience that going limbless is bad for your mental health. Prolonged isolation, loneliness, and depression are often the result of amputees not being able to wear their legs. As I get older, I know these types of sores are going to happen and one day I'll be using crutches or perhaps a wheelchair in the library. Sores in all their variations are a byproduct of when artificial limbs meet human flesh. It's gotten better, much better.

As we talked I saw some of my old books that I had read, donated, and helped catalog earlier this summer. They are not brand new, but when books are new to us, we feature them on the new shelves with "new" stickers. *Who Says I Can't* and *Drinking from My Leg*, two books by amputees were sitting on the shelf.

"I could feel something, but I had to get a mirror to look at the back of my stump." When your leg is trapped in a canister, heated to a boiling point here in the South, sometimes it's hard to tell when something is uncomfortable or has already gone horribly wrong. Sores, blisters, and open wounds can be caused by something as simple as a rumpled sock, or something more complex like a change in physical mass of your leg that results in an ill-fitting socket.

"I went to the wound care at Thomas Hospital," Paul said.

"They deal mostly with diabetes patients there, don't they?" I wondered if they were any help.

"I was hoping they were going to have a magic elixir to heal the wound faster and all they gave me was this ridiculous Band-

Aid," he said, and we were both laughing as he spaced out a half inch between his thumb and forefinger. He was looking for a balm, the kind Jackie Chiles warned Cosmo Kramer about in *Seinfeld*. "You put the balm on? Who told you to put the balm on?" When I was a kid and sores forced me to go artificial limbless, my mom always went for the "medicated ointment" in the square, green tin can. Similar in consistency to Vaseline, Bag Balm claims to reduce and relieve irritations and moisturize a cow's udders.

"You never know what a balm is gonna do," Jackie cautioned. Balms are unpredictable. Sometimes the Bag Balm worked, sometimes it didn't.

"The doctor said it'll be at least another ten days." I realized that the patrons staring at Paul were completely oblivious to the fact that we share similar circumstances. We both need a below the knee prosthesis to walk around.

We vowed to do a better job of self-examinations to make sure our stump skin is healthy.

Out of the corner of my eye, I saw a woman at a public computer station raising one hand and finger-curling me over with another. I nodded, and looked back at Paul and apologized for having to cut the conversation short.

"Thanks for coming in today," I told him, "and take care of yourself." I touched his shoulder and hoped he felt my reassurance.

I wanted to share my news with Paul that I am teaching English 101 at the University of Mobile. I didn't. It seemed more important to listen and share information about our less-than-four lot in life. Most amputees, including myself, have been where Paul stands: on one leg, waiting impatiently for a wound to heal. What I didn't realize is that he's in his 70s. He's still running in his 70s. Another trait I share with my sitcom brother is that, "I choose not to run." I can run, and do so as long as there is a purpose. I'm not one of these 5K people. I need to be chasing something, a ball, "it" in tag. Or, I run if someone's chasing me.

Until he can put his leg on again, Paul has other qualities that will help him through this trial, like patience, persistence, and perseverance. In other words, like the name of the novel and movie, the man has *True Grit*.

Osseointegration at Orange Beach

I went to the Orange Beach Public Library after our bloggers meeting. I was on a mission for a print version of a journal for library school homework. I thought, for some reason, if anyone had a copy it would be Louise, who graduated from Alabama three years ago. She's a dedicated, energetic, and innovative librarian so I stopped in to say hello.

She was talking with a guy when I walked over to her desk.

After becoming reacquainted, I handed over a copy of my assignment and said, "I'm looking for a copy of this," pointing to the title.

"Oh JASIST. I know exactly what journal you mean," Louise said, the familiarity of the assignment now as fresh in her mind as it was five years ago.

I was in my shorts, having just come from a swim in the Gulf. The entire time Louise and I were talking the guy was staring at my prosthesis, a typical occurrence with children, but odd behavior for an adult.

"I'm Rick," he interrupted us, barely lifting his eyes up to meet mine.

"Alan," I said, and we shook hands.

He wasn't bashful, that's for sure, as he blurted out a question about how my prosthesis is attached.

"Is your prosthesis connected to bone?"

"No," I said, "that's someone who's gone through osseointegration, a surgery that is still unapproved in the United States."

Osseointegration is a surgery that leaves a metal rod sticking out of your stump where a prosthesis can be attached.

Anyway, this guy Rick seemed a bit obsessed, so much so that he was distracting me from my conversation with Louise. I wondered how well Louise knew this patron. She probably wondered why he was so fixated on my prosthesis. I'm used to talking about my leg, but other amputees prefer not to discuss it. There are all kinds of odd behavior in the able-bodied and amputee world. Acrotomophilia is when an individual expresses strong sexual interest in amputees and are called amputee devotees. Other people suffer from apotemnophilia, a sexual desire to have a perfectly healthy limb amputated.

"I met a guy who had a prosthesis attached to his bone," he said.

"Really," I said, not sure if I should believe him.

"The guy was in the service," Rick said.

"I just threw out a copy at home," Louise said.

Then she went to the stacks behind her desk, "I weeded that one too."

I suggested she check her boss's office, not realizing he was not in today.

"He keeps it locked, and he wouldn't have a copy anyway," she said, and headed off to check somewhere else in the library.

"Are you gonna have the surgery?"

"No, I think it's for younger people." I didn't tell him I was a better candidate for osteoporosis than osseointegration.

"The veteran told me it gets infected a lot and he takes medications to control the infection. Hey, is that titanium?" Rick asked, pointing below the socket.

"No, that's an alloy, but my old leg has titanium hardware," I explained.

When I got home, I looked at the literature I had on file for osseointegration. Rick, it turns out, was more credible than I gave him credit for. As I dug through my files I found the information for a clinical trial and an article on Miranda Cashin, an Aussie who underwent the procedure and blogged about it from 2012 to 2014. Cashin initially thought of the procedure as "science fiction—I would essentially become a Cyborg."

As for Rick, well, who would have guessed two patrons in a public library could share such an obscure interest. It's more than a coincidence, it's serendipitous! You never know where the next leg is going to come from or who you are going to meet in a public library.

9. Reference-Literary Legs

T. "The sole member of your audience will probably be some desperately lonely old male librarian who saw a light in the window of the lecture hall and hopefully came in to escape the cold and the horrors of his personal hell. There in the hall, his stooped figure sitting alone before the podium, your nasal voice echoing among the empty chairs and hammering boredom, confusion, and sexual reference deeper and deeper into the poor wretch's bald skull, confounded to the point of hysteria, he will doubtlessly exhibit himself, waving his crabbed organ like a club in despair against the grim sound that drones on and on over his head."

At the desk, in Jillian Crochet's crocheted skullcap.

Walking Aids

They lean against the wall next to the bed.
No laminate, press, or particle board.
Real pine, circa 1989.
Galvanized, not stainless steel, screws and wing nuts
Hold my sticks together.
Frames with adjustable pegs for height and hand holders.
Underarm and hand grip pads are original software
Still smelling better than my stump after a day
In a carbon fiber socket in the Lower Alabama humidity.

The empty leg leans against Grandma's rocker
Titanium hardware clamps carbon fiber
foot, post, and socket together.
Allen wrench screws tightened after a
Dip in Loctite 242 Blue.
A new rechargeable vacuum,
with blue tooth capability,
strapped to the post with zip ties,
keeps my gel-lined stump sucked
securely into a diamond-plated socket.

Melville and Ahab

The images of leg loss in 19th century fiction typically ignore a character's prosthetic history or amputee experience. Authors often portray those with leg loss as villains, or the butt of jokes. Unfortunately, fiction is the source of much of the knowledge the world holds about limb loss. However, contemporary authors who have real-life experience with one-legged-ness are now using their personal knowledge of disability to create compelling characters and narratives.

According to introductory notes to *Moby Dick* by Carl Hovde, Herman Melville's Captain Ahab, in the Shakespearean tradition of tragedy, "is a great man brought down by his faults." He adds that "Ahab had to be built from the ground up as a man worthy of great regard." Melville intentionally hides Ahab and readers don't know about his disability until Captain Peleg (who ironically has two good legs) tells Ishmael, "Clap eye on Captain Ahab...and though wilt find that he has only one leg."

The most iconic image in *Moby Dick* is Ahab's appearance on deck for the first time, commanding his ship while his peg rests in the augered hole of the quarterdeck. Ishmael, the narrator, describes the "barbaric white leg.... His bone leg steadied in that hole; one arm elevated, and holding by a shroud; Captain Ahab stood erect, looking straight out beyond the ship's ever-pitching prow." Ahab is angry and bent on revenge, two of the most powerful human emotions.

Disability Studies is an area of study and political activity that focuses attention on the disability experience, a way of life for an estimated 15 percent of the US population. Most people will become disabled at least once in their lives due to injury or as part of the aging process. Many scholars in the emerging field of Disability Studies focus on physical and mental disability as an identity and also a literary construct. Thomas Couser writes, "Disability is an inescapable element of human existence and experience." According to David Mitchell, "the irony is that people with disabilities were never officially identified as a social collectivity or cultural minority," a situation that gave Melville and others like him the ability to represent physical differences in any manner they saw fit.

Melville emphasizes the physicality of Ahab, including the necessary accommodations that have been made for Ahab to move aboard the ship. The narrator describes, for example, Ahab "gripping the iron banister, to help his crippled way" or the noisy "crack and din of his bony step." He notes that the deck planks "were all over dented, like geological stones, with the peculiar mark of his walk." Ahab is so full of rage he vows to "dismember my dismemberer." For the harpooning boat Ahab added an "extra coat of sheathing...to withstand the pointed pressure of his ivory limb." A semicircular depression was carved into the boat to cradle the knee and take weight off the peg while he stood in the bow, harpoon in hand.

A few pages later we get this wonderfully dramatic sound from Ahab's peg: "The live leg made lively echoes," while "every stroke of his dead limb sounded like a coffin-tap." The reader, listening carefully, can hear the dreadful yet symbolic thud as Ahab paces the deck while foreshadowing the coffin making for Queequeg and its use as a life preserver by Ishmael. Melville also uses repetition to bring us aside Ahab, and he does it when Ahab's on deck and his "ivory leg inserted into his accustomed hole, and with one hand firmly grasping a shroud." Later, the reader sees Ahab in action again with wonderful verb choice as he "revolved in his pivot hole," and in that instant the reader spins with the captain. It's worth noting that Melville describes how *Moby Dick* "reaped" Ahab's leg, "as a mower a blade of grass in the field." Coincidentally, the motorized mower blades of today still account for lost legs and feet.

The crew jokes about Ahab's leg, but the sailors also consider levels of disability. "If I had but one leg," Stubb tells Flask, "you would not catch me in a boat, unless maybe to stop the plug hole with my timber toe." After the joke, Flask defends his captain's physical ability. "If his leg were off at the hip, now, it would be a different thing. That would disable him; but he has one knee, and good part of the other left." The distinction drawn between types of leg loss and how disability or ability is defined varies even among able-bodied whale men.

In the chapter "Leg and Arm," Ahab meets the one-armed captain of the *Samuel Enderby*, Captain Boomer, and confronts another physical obstacle. Ahab, unaccustomed to leaving his ship on a peg, has to be lifted onto the deck to meet with Boomer, "using a massive curbed blubber hook." In the scene Ahab "slid his solitary thigh into the curve of the hook (it was like sitting in the fluke of the anchor, or the crotch of an apple tree).... and at the same time also helped to hoist his own weight" so the two captains can "shake bones together."

In "Ahab's Leg," although the peg rests in the hole, "the additional twist and wrench" of the peg leads Ahab to "deem it entirely untrustworthy" and orders the ship's carpenter to make a new peg of "jaw ivory" and "iron contrivances." A carpenter and a blacksmith on board are not only there for whaling purposes, but they are there to build Ahab a new leg. This is an insightful component to Melville's writing because we see that the leg doesn't last forever: labor and material are required to keep Ahab moving.

Ishmael is frequently staring at Ahab and making observations or remembering scenes about leg loss. By looking back into Melville's life and writings, readers can see that Melville, like Ishmael, has a fascination with whaling and disability, specifically leg loss. In the description of the "crippled beggar," Ishmael recalls seeing a man without a peg begging for money who "exhibited that stump to an incredulous world." Melville calls the Navy an "asylum for the perverse, the home of the unfortunate." Ishmael's view of the beggar is juxtaposed with his knowledge of Ahab, the revenge-seeking Captain, who is the exception to the stereotype; the man begging on the docks is the cultural norm. Men who go to sea often go because their appearances do not suit the larger society in which they find themselves. It was not uncommon for sailors, pirates, and officers to travel the high seas with fewer than four limbs, but Ahab as the captain was still an exception.

While it is true that "Historically, then, disability has been represented primarily by non-disabled writers and almost exclusively in fictive or imaginative genres" readers should not conclude that there is no representational value in those earlier works for the contemporary reader or writer who is disabled.

Melville's inspiration for Ahab comes from his experience sailing aboard the *Acushnet* whaling ship, where he observed Captain Pease treating his men badly. While serving on the *Acushnet* Melville was given a book to read by William Henry Chase, son of Owen Chase, the man who survived the Essex shipwreck. An avid researcher, Melville read with great interest, and later met George Pollard, a Nantucket resident and captain of the *Essex*. Charles Wilkes, a naval officer and explorer who ran a tight ship and disciplined his men heavy-handedly, is said to be another model for Melville's characterization of Ahab. Both men had two good legs. Disability Scholar Samuel Otter writes, "From the very start of his writing career, Melville was fascinated with human variation and mutability, by ideas about norms and the facts of divergence."

Melville wrote an essay for *Yankee Doodle* about P. T. Barnum's American Museum and its display of General Antonio López de Santa Anna's prosthetic leg (Taylor 1). Disability Studies authors David Mitchell and Sharon Snyder stress the paradoxical view that the social and cultural invisibility of disabled people "has occurred in the wake of their perpetual circulation throughout print history." Melville takes this artifact and uses stereotypical writing when he writes about Santa Anna's prosthetic leg on display at the hugely popular museum and Ishmael's cultural representation of the "beggar" in *Moby Dick*. Melville's Ahab is represented as a physically limited character, but this does not prevent him from captaining a ship. Melville overexposes how disability is represented.

Baynton writes that "Humans use metaphor and mental imagery to understand things of which they have no direct experience." We can see how Melville developed his characters to reflect his experiences and observations. Literary narratives are often constructed around life experiences and therefore depend on nonfiction material. Melville took scraps of information from various sources through observation. A shipmate detail, excess ivory, a strange limp, or an odd movement helped to shape Melville's captain and Ahab's leg. Melville merged a marginalized character like the beggar with Santa Anna's leg and gave the world the first representational view of a one-legged man.

Stevenson and Long John Silver

Another author who based a fictional character on a real person is Robert Louis Stevenson. He based *Treasure Island*, an often-autobiographical adventure story of piracy, on his childhood memories. In this coming-of-age story, Stevenson incorporates his own experience into the character of the novel's protagonist, Jim Hawkins. In this classic young adult novel, Stevenson strips his main character, Long John Silver, of his leg, and props him up with a crutch.

In Stevenson's novel, Silver is foil to Hawkins, a contrasting character of devious and questionable qualities. Squire Trelawney tells the story that Silver lost his leg "in his country's service." Later Israel Hand praises Silver's "good schooling" and vouches that he is as "brave" as a lion. Silver is conniving and manipulative and Stevenson brings a ruthlessness, vulnerability, and complexity to his one-legged pirate, but he does something more. In creating Silver, Stevenson, an admitted pirate himself who plagiarized plot ideas from several authors to tell his pirate tale, understood the importance of observation when writing about physical appearance and movement. Stevenson gives an accurate description using details of how Silver learned to use the "old timber I hobble on."

Stevenson's friend, poet William E. Henley, was the primary inspiration for Silver, the crutch-wielding sea cook. Both men lived with a disability. Suffering from tuberculosis, or consumption, Stevenson had chronic lung problems and other ailments that kept him bedridden for long stretches throughout his life (including the period during which he wrote what would become *Treasure Island*). Henley's left leg was amputated below the knee. The two men met in 1873 when Henley was hospitalized in an effort to save his other foot from amputation. Henley wrote his most famous poem, "Invictus," while still hospitalized in 1875. The poem was first published without a title in Henley's *A Book of Verse* and later given the title "Invictus," or unconquered. The two men were writing collaborators and Henley worked as agent and editor to advance Stevenson's writing career for more than a decade.

In *Treasure Island*, Hawkins tells us of his encounters with Silver in great detail. "His *left* (emphasis added) leg was cut off close by the hip, and under the left shoulder he carried a crutch, which he managed with wonderful dexterity, hopping about upon it like a bird." In *Moby Dick*, Flask says of Ahab: "his leg were cut off at the hip...that would disable him." Hawkins's favorable impression of Silver's overcoming his disability contrasts with Flask's view of a person with disabilities. Later, the reader is told that Silver "carried his crutch by a lanyard round his neck to keep both hands free." To further aid his mobility on deck "Long John's earrings," were strung up like a clothes line around the ship. Rather than crutch around, Silver used "a line or two rigged up" on the decks so he could move more easily from place to place. Stevenson not only brings Silver to life but he sets him in constant motion on the deck when he writes, "He would hand himself from one place to another, now using the crutch, now trailing it alongside by the lanyard, as quickly as another man could walk."

In May 1883, shortly after *Treasure Island* was published, Stevenson wrote Henley: "I will now make a confession. It was the sight of your maimed strength and masterfulness that begot John Silver in *Treasure Island*.... The idea of the maimed man, ruling and dreaded by the sound, was entirely taken from you." The value of Stevenson's portrayal of disability is immense since such perspectives were rare in the 19th century.

Critics and editors make leg loss portrayal worse when they misidentify or trivialize Silver in their erroneous description of the crutch-wielding sea cook turned captain. The inside jacket of Clare Harman's book, *Myself and the Other Fellow: A Life of Robert Louis Stevenson*, describes Silver with a "wooden leg." In the section "Inspired by *Treasure Island*" by Angus Fletcher, Silver is the "archetypal peg-legged pirate" (243). The pirate Stevenson created had neither. Silver used "with wonderful dexterity" (58), and innovation, a crude wooden crutch. There are obvious distinctions between a peg leg, a crude crutch-like post, a wooden leg that has a foot and is shaped like a leg, and a man without a leg leaning on one crutch for his mobility. Readers should consider how difficult it is to ambulate with one leg using just a single crutch. It requires tremendous upper body strength and asymmetrical balance. The peg leg was a modified version of the crutch that was specifically meant to free up both hands. This distinction is important for Silver, known by his fellow pirates as Barbecue. Perhaps Stevenson chose to portray Silver without a leg subconsciously because of his own disability and bedridden youth or by mirroring his friend Henley.

In the chapter "Silver's Embassy," Silver is sitting on the ground outside the fort with Captain Smollet, who refuses to give the treasure map to Silver and further demands that the pirates surrender. When negotiations reach an impasse, the one-legged pirate asks for a hand up so he can rise from the ground, but none is given. This is the contradiction many amputees find themselves in: they want to be treated the same, and yet they are different. They require assistance at times. This complication is the essence of Silver's character. Perhaps a similar experience was witnessed by Stevenson in the treatment of people with disabilities. Stevenson is said to have carried Henley on numerous occasions out of a hospital bed to an awaiting carriage for their outings. Stevenson later wrote about how he used Henley as a model for Silver.

"To take an admired friend of mine (whom the reader very likely knows and admires as much as I do), to deprive him of all his finer qualities and higher graces of temperament, to leave him with nothing but his strength, his courage, his quickness, and his magnificent geniality, and to try to express these in terms of the culture of a raw tarpaulin." (Stevenson 77-78)

He elaborates on the writer's use of real people in the creation of characters:

"Psychical surgery is, I think, a common way of 'making character'; perhaps it is, indeed, the only way. We can put in the quaint figure that spoke a hundred words with us yesterday by the wayside; but do we know him? Our friend, with his infinite variety and flexibility, we know - but can we put him in…. knife in hand, we must cut away and deduct the needless arborescence of his nature, but the trunk and the few branches that remain we may at least be fairly sure of." (Stevenson 77-78)

As with trees, a character can be identified, has a certain structure, and grows. Stevenson limns the soul or trunk of Henley and uses his imagination to graft Silver to Henley's lower limbs.

In a comment about his research for his literary Disability Studies doctoral research, University of Leicester's Dr. Thomas Coogan writes, "Impairment makes itself known through writing, even when the authors don't consciously identify themselves as disabled." Stevenson used Henley to portray

Silver, but how much, given Coogan's suggestion, is Stevenson writing about his own disability? Does Stevenson identify with Henley so much that he masks or mixes his own physical disability with Henley's? Coogan underscores the legitimacy of Stevenson's mixing of his own disability with that of his friend. By peeling back the layer of this young adult novel, originally published in *Young Folks* magazine as "The Sea Cook," readers can see the complexities of Stevenson's actual relationship with Henley. Silver's story, mirroring Henley's disability experience, provides a fresh perspective on how amputees are represented in fiction.

Emily Rapp: Ambivalence and Identity

The focus of Emily Rapp's book, *Poster Child: A Memoir*, is the author's conflicting feelings, her ambivalence about the loss of her left leg. *The Oxford English Dictionary* defines ambivalence as "the coexistence in one person of contradictory emotions or attitudes (as love or hatred) towards a person or thing." *The Gale Encyclopedia of Psychology* further defines ambivalence as "the concurrent existence...of contrasting, opposing, or contradictory feelings, emotions, or attitudes." *Merriam-Webster's Dictionary* also defines ambivalence as a contrast in "actions." Early on, Rapp uses ambivalence in her characterization of people.

As the "poster child" for the March of Dimes in the Midwest, she was depicted as the cute little girl in pigtails who overcame her disability. As Rapp writes, as she got older, she wrestled with issues of loss, identity, and body image as she tried to come to terms with her birth defect and subsequent leg amputation.

Rapp conveys in her memoir the complex and often contradictory feelings amputees grapple with, but she also provides insight into how others perceive those with limb differences. Rapp's fleeting fame as poster child does not translate to positive body image when she becomes a teen or later as an adult. Rapp uses ambivalence in her writing to convey her own feelings about herself and towards her stump, prosthesis, body image, and ultimately her very identity.

Shortly after Rapp was born, the doctors discovered her abnormality. Her mother told her that the nurse gave her a look that Rapp would later come to know as "a look of pity, sadness, with kindness and a bit of unexplainable triumph mixed in." In reflecting on her parents hearing the news of her disability,

215

proximal focal femoral deficiency, she considers their mixed emotions in learning the bad news after the elation of being told about and seeing what they thought was a healthy baby. Rapp interestingly, and perhaps intentionally, withholds the detail that it was her left leg that was affected by the deficiency until after she names the disorder. Rapp reflects on the roller coaster of emotions her parents experience when she writes, "After a long and difficult labor, all had been declared normal, then abnormal."

The book's prologue begins with Rapp facing mechanical problems with her prosthesis while she is a Fulbright scholar teaching young students in Korea. While walking down the street, Rapp's hydraulic knee malfunctions, she loses her balance, and as the "left leg buckled beneath" she "fell backward into a puddle of motor oil." As she composes herself in front of a street vendor she notices people are staring, a foreshadowing of her fear and uncertainty throughout the book of an unstable prosthesis. Every amputee knows that, just like anything mechanical, artificial parts break and they are faced with the challenges of repair in order for mobility to be restored. When they do break, there is this feeling among amputees, a sort of sixth sense, that warns us in a combination of sound and feeling that something on our manmade device has broken.

Amputees have to be aware of their natural bodies but there is also the burden of knowing and maintaining the artificial parts. A night of babysitting as a teenager also turns into a dramatic prosthetic failure. "I was chasing her around the corner when I felt something catch in my ankle followed by a soft cracking noise ... and then the foot was spinning around as easily as a merry go round on its axis." Rapp expresses her mixed feelings about pain, body image and how it relates to her disability and her prosthesis. Shortly after her amputation, "The pain of nostalgia" is how she describes her phantom limb pain. The dichotomy of the negative connotations of pain and the positive, often pleasant perception of the word nostalgia is unique.

The scene where she dives into the pool for the first time when she is seven years old is an example of the importance of motion and movement in water, which is so therapeutic and physically freeing for many amputees. "I felt absorbed, taken under, and enveloped.... My body felt light and remarkably even, its asymmetry balanced and supported by the softness of the water." There is a sense of belonging in the water, a feeling of naturalness for the author that stems from a childhood memory and an everlasting sense of accomplishment. "The fin on my right foot made me feel like a fish cutting gracefully through the water." Remembering how it felt to swim for the first time after the amputation, she continues, "I was dividing a space with my body versus being divided: by a surgeon, by a prosthetist, by a wooden leg that was removed each night and lay by my bed until morning." It should be noted that the whole experience also drew stares from people young and old at the pool. On this particular day, Rapp felt empowered by her body and the things it could do despite its imperfections and the continuous stares from strangers.

One way amputees get to the bigger picture is through dialogue with others and internal conversations with themselves. Rapp reflects on the questions her mother might have asked herself, "Will she walk, run, skip, play, read and write?" Questions directed at the author include the always popular, "What happened to your leg?" These questions echo throughout her book, but the answers are not always provided.

Couser points out that in the last three decades the most significant development of memoir writing has been "the proliferation of book-length accounts (from both the first and third person points of view) of living with illness and disability." Today there are multiple representations of disabling conditions. Couser explains that autobiography is proliferating because "life writing by disabled people is a cultural manifestation of a human rights movement," which in the United States has come on the heels of the 1970s disability rights movement and the passage of the Americans with Disabilities Act in 1990.

Poet Kenny Fries writes, "Throughout history, people with disabilities have been stared at …. Now…. writers with disabilities affirm our lives by putting the world on notice that we are staring back." Fries' book *Staring Back* is a collection of fiction, nonfiction, poetry, and drama that is "the product of a disabled writer's encounter with his or her own disability experience … told from the perspective of a writer who lives with disabilities." For writers, there is a vast difference between life writing, autobiography or memoir, and "the collaborative effort" or ghostwritten-as-told-to books circulating. According to Couser, the latter "seems to require less in the way of literary expertise and experience." More books about the disabled experience are being published without "the condition that the narrative take a story of triumph" and without regard to gender.

Rapp also wrestles with her body image during her first sexual encounter. While a student in Dublin, she meets Luke and before sleeping with him, struggles with what to do with her above knee prosthesis. "How would it work? Would I be able to easily manipulate the leg or would the knee lock out at embarrassing moments and inhibit my movements?" Despite encouragement from a friend to take the leg off for the occasion, Rapp writes, "to remove the leg in front of a man was unthinkable; the very thought of it sickened me. I had no sense of myself as a desirable, sexual woman as an amputee." She adds, "When it was attached, I felt like a complete person; when it was removed I felt monstrous and deformed." The action of taking the leg on and off and the feelings resulting from that creates intense ambivalence. Later she gives what she calls her "poster child speech" to Luke, which included just the happy highlights and the triumph over adversity. The most telling line about the whole experience was not what happened or how, but the dishonesty between the couple about her disability. "We both pretended it didn't exist, that everything was normal."

Later in a second rendezvous with Luke in Chicago she is undressing in the bathroom. After taking off her prosthesis she writes, "The stump was hideous; it was scarred and disgusting – even penis resembling." Her decision shortly after this to question the "dissonance" between her self-image and her true feelings led her to study her disability as a theological issue. What she discovers is that other disabled women share her struggles about body, image, and identity. In a small group with other disabled women from around the world, Rapp finally emerges from the poster child image of herself, revealing to the group of deeply religious women, "I have always hated my body." She calls the group a "sisterhood – unspoken but felt – that I had never experienced before." It is through her depiction of this shared community that readers begin to understand the author's struggle of body image, difference and identity. About her body, Rapp explains it was "a place I inhabited but felt disconnected from at the same time." She says, "It is mine." Rapp's ambivalence advances lost leg literature into the modern century, and her rising self-awareness and identity provides a new model for disability writing.

Jillian Weise: Body Image and Art

The Amputee's Guide to Sex, a poetry collection by Jillian Weise, is not a "how to" manual for amputees, exactly, but it offers her personal perspectives on leg loss. It also gives away secrets about how those with malformed bodies seek to hide their differences from their partners. At times those attempts inject some humor into the story, especially during awkward intimate moments. We learn how experience, discovery, and reflection shaped her life and perceptions of her body and how men, especially, treated her differently because of her leglessness. The fear of intimate situations with non-disabled individuals can be devastating to a disabled person's psyche.

In the section of the poetry collection titled, "Translating the Body," Weise uses powerful images to connect her own experiences as an amputee and amputee history with art and architecture. In the poem "Abscission," her reference to the construction of the Taj Mahal resonates with her own feelings about her disabilities: "the emperor ordered a mass amputation of thumbs / so the craftsmen could never build / a more perfect mausoleum." In another poem she makes comparisons to the duality of beauty and bodies. After her lover takes off his clothes in the poem "Notes on the Body," Weise writes, "I see the Statue of David." And in "Half Portrait," she dreams, "Mona Lisa into a wheelchair."

Weise uses images of freakery, fetishes, questions, and aquatic themes to depict her missing leg. In the poem "Below Water," she approaches the stigma of a damaged body. "Below water, I kick one and a half / legs, pretend to be a mermaid." What missing-limbed or able-bodied person has not dreamt of looking differently? In contrast, the last two lines read, "I wish we could always be / a horizon of faces, hidden bodies." In the poem, "During the Reign of Alter Ego," there is a nod to people who prey on the disabled and those with "Fake Leg Fetishes." There are people, both men and women, who stalk those with less than four limbs. For example, in "Beautiful Freak Show," the one-legged narrator describes being seen naked by a landlord "peeking from a hole in the closet wall," into her room as a man in the room asks her to "pivot and pose, unstrap the leg." This physical and psychosexual struggle for identity is evident but she knows of other ways to further devalue her body when she writes, "You think I care for / this body? Watch." There is an authenticity to Weise's poems that amputee readers can identify with from having similar experiences. This is most evident in "The Old Questions," a poem about the most commonly asked questions of amputees. "Will you show me your leg? Do you sleep with it on? Do you bathe with it on? Is it all right if I touch it?"

In "Fragments" questions are posed that resonate with people with disabilities, beginning with "Don't you wish you had both legs?" This line of questioning, similar to Emily Rapp's queries, is a way to mine a deeper conundrum: how to represent one's identity authentically but also honestly respond to the stereotypes of leg loss expressed by one's intimate partners.

The title of one section, "Of Holman," is a homophone for "whole man," a play on words that refers to the non-disabled person and humanity in general. In these poems, Weise addresses both the physical body she inhabits and her relationship to language. In the epilogue "Body as Argument," she refers to the ambivalence of an intimate relationship with a man: "we have been sleeping together for three months without ever taking each other's clothes off." There is a connection between what is not said and what is unseen with both Weise and Rapp. In "The Gift" Weise humorously imagines getting a "real, live leg" transplant in Louisville, Kentucky, while her boyfriend gets a "better" penis, "less veiny, more girth."

Identity is constantly challenged and compromised as in the poem "Subversive." She is being blackmailed by a young "Holman" who vows that he will "take me to the Valentine's Dance / if I let him take off the stockings / and foam to hear the knee creak." Weise's disability is construed as a sign of weakness for the able-bodied to prey upon.

Weise leaves out a significant detail in her poetry. The reader is never told which leg was amputated. Is the detail necessary? Readers could conclude that she is a hip-disarticulate amputee. She has kept this and the specifics of her spine surgery private, choosing to let her poetry speak for the pain. Weise and Rapp are attempting to "craft a self out of words," according to Carl Klaus in *The Made-Up Self: Impersonation in the Personal Essay*. Weise's poem, "Conviction," creates a character without a leg as a way to express isolation and difference. She writes, "I'm convinced we both take off / our legs and put them on each morning." It's possible she's writing about herself at two different times or she has created an imaginary friend that shares her disability.

The "I" in the poem may be Weise as a child; she is perhaps sharing or comparing memory with her present-day self when she writes "your leg is a newer/model, foam and titanium." A transformation takes place, according to Patricia Foster, who writes in Klaus's book, as when "the delicate moments in novels are fascinating and compelling because they are the most revealing of the interior self, of the human psyche." Foster adds, "like the novel and poetry, the personal essay is...looking at the cross-purposes of the psyche, the human heart, yet moving one step closer to experience by its use of the first person singular." For Weise this is evident in her poem, "Training Wheels," when the silence of forbidden words like "handicap or different or special" was broken by her grandfather.

> When I hopped to the bathroom,
> he shouted, Prettiest cripple I ever
> seen and I woke everyone up yelling
> Am not, am not, am not!
>
> My father walked out of his bedroom
> to the refrigerator and said, what did
> you do? as if it were my fault
> I looked in the full-length mirror
>
> at the shadow of one leg
> Beneath a nightgown. (13-22)

This poem for amputees is the pinnacle. Readers watch as worlds collide and the family that seeks to protect and shelter Weise from meanness and cruelty falters. Tragically, what Weise takes from this is that not only is her identity different but now as she looks at her image in the mirror, she is to blame for the family conflict.

Weise's autobiographical poetry, told from varying viewpoints about leg loss, is a type of disability life writing. This approach provides both a sword and shield for Weise in terms of how she portrays her persona on the page. Weise offers readers a lesson in literary dissonance. Her multiple authentic self-representations and points of view contrast with her poetic distances and imaginative lenses.

10. Memorials

U. "That's all I want is my leg back. It feels like I lost my leg all over again. My limb. My actual limb. This is how it felt, you know. And I don't understand what they're going to do with it."

Looking at some photos with Mom,
Falmouth, Massachusetts

Library Tip:

If you want your name to be in your public library's catalog, but have no intention of writing a book, make a donation! Most libraries, when donations are given for the purchase of books, in memory of someone for instance, librarians catalog the book. Catalogers include in the MARC (Machine Readable Cataloging) record both the person who is being remembered and the donor. Donors can then search the OPAC (Online Public Access Catalog), using their name or the memorial name, and voila! Your name shows up in your library's catalog. And, more importantly, you've helped your library's collection development.

Where's Mom?

It's been over a month since my mom died. I still occasionally find myself driving over to her apartment after work to visit. Sometimes I'll want to tell her something. To reach her these days, I need a completely different vehicle.

***

I found a nice spot on the Fish River, a small park, under a canopy of cedar, magnolia, pine, and live oak.

It's quiet, clear, and sunny with gusts from the west blowing overhead, with an occasional swirl upriver. Pollen, leaves, catkins, and pine needles float by on the river current.

A brown magnolia leaf, curved just right, keel down and canoe-shaped like it was made just for the water, is lifted off the shoreline by the river.

It's floating for the current, closer to the far side of the river, but slowly. Now, it's outside of the swiftest part of the current but moving closer to it. Finally, the leaf is collected into the fast flow. I watch it as it rounds the bend. I don't know how far it's going to make it.

Maybe the leaf will float all the way to my coworker Danielle's house, near the confluence of the Fish River and Weeks Bay.

Then again, I suspect another stretch of river, where it is wide, deep, and rough, will capsize Mother Earth's canoe. Once capsized, she'll rock back and forth cradle-like through the water until she rests on the bottom, joining the leaves from springs of yesteryear.

227

As I lift my head up to enjoy the scenery, I jump out of my seat...scared by a shadow of a red-tailed hawk. Now that I'm up I wander around the shoreline a bit. The water is clear closest to the river bank, thanks to the sandy bottom. Minnows flinch from nibbling at my footstep, and dance away with one another, and then return.

With a hand on a cedar, I gaze at the water and see a bubble, not a ripple from a fish kissing the surface, but a small bubble, rising from the darker, black bottom. I walk closer. From below the layer of leaves, sticks, and decomposing black river bottom, two more bubbles rise. Freshwater mussel? Crawfish? Whatever it is, it's so happy to be alive in the river's dead organic matter, it sends up three more bubbles.

Returning to my seat I notice another magnolia leaf is gathered up by the river. It moves upriver for several yards, and is caught in an eddy, not far from the bubbles. The leaf circles, circles faster on the second spin, and catches the main current. I decide to stay and watch a few more leaf launchings.

***

Mom and I enjoyed our visit along the river. We had a nice conversation too. I sent leaf letters and she replied in word bubbles.

11. Vertical File

V. "An act of imagination is an act of self-acceptance."

An alphabetized file of pamphlets, small publications, clippings, and ephemera that is maintained and kept in a file cabinet to answer brief questions or to provide points of information but does not merit a call number in a library system.

Knoll Park, Fairhope, my first outdoor writing experiment.

Making and Breaking Records

I decided to go to the Mobile Writer's Guild Drink-n-Scrawl. A chance to get out, write with other writers, and drink sounded good. I especially appreciated the event's word order. I heard about it word-of-finger; a friend posted it on her social networking site. I marked the date in my Moleskine calendar, went to the Writer's Guild web page, and clicked "Attend."

Leading up to the date, I thought about giving the other writers something to write about by leaving my prosthetic leg at home. The idea of going prosthesis-free came after I read a quote in *The Seattle Times* about a high school girl who was missing parts of all four limbs. Kiera Brinkley danced without prosthetics on her stumps. She said, "It lets people see the real me." As I was trying to wrap my head around such a profound statement from a high school girl who is clearly more mature than my 42 years, I started to question my own identity.

Could I crutch into the Mellow Mushroom in Midtown Mobile? Yes, and I decided to use the event not just as a social experiment, but also to help answer a recent personal question raised by the one-legged woman I'd seen at the library. At home, I'm comfortable crutching around the house, but taking this private persona public left me excited and apprehensive. Am I more me with the leg on or off?

Then it hit me. Walking out of the house—as opposed to crutching—had become routine. I couldn't recall the last time I went out in public without a fake leg on. My wife, Susan, couldn't remember the last time I went out in public on crutches either. Crutches are things and yet I use the word as a verb. I crutch into the kitchen. The crutches are crippling both visually and physically. The stigma attached to crutches is that

230

you need a walking aid for mobility. Walking with a limp or a hitch goes unnoticed, or at least minimally noticed, but crutches are a symbol of infirmity, like someone waving a white flag on the battlefield. Could I block out the stares, answer questions, and still write? I vowed to leave my prosthesis home and go out into the world—to drink and write.

"What's the record?" Susan asks. Do other amputees track this type of thing? Perhaps I have set two new records. Consecutive days of wearing a prosthesis in public. Consecutive days of crutching around the house. The last time I went out in public with crutches was 21 years ago. I've been married for 19 years.

The "pitfalls" (pun intended) for crutch users are many. A recent *InMotion* magazine article, "An Overview of Crutches" by Madeleine Anderson, could not have spelled it out any clearer to me. "No matter how conscientious you are, leaning with your whole weight on the crutch tops will result in peripheral nerve damage." Crutches are now regarded as unhealthy. How? "Hard on shoulders... make you hunch over leading to bad posture and back aches" (47). The hand grips can produce carpal tunnel syndrome. Here's the kicker though. Anderson says, "Sometimes this damage will not show up for years."

How come I've never heard this before? I work at a reference/information desk, after all. I love my old wooden underarm crutches. Once I'm comfortable with something, I just love to limp along. Not quite in the Stone-Age but my crutch choice is Egyptian. The crutch dates back to ancient Egypt. Servants designed them for pharaohs using branches of trees or carved them from wood and padded the tops for underarm support and better comfort. In 1917, Emile Shlick patented an early walking stick with an underarm support. A.R. Lofstrand Jr. went a step further with his forearm crutch. The

Lofstrand crutch is used by slipping an arm into the forearm cuff. In 1945, Lofstrand filed a patent that made his forearm cuff adjustable to the height of the user.

The subheading of the article says, "Crutches have evolved." These wooden ones I ponder retiring were a parting gift from Dr. Kruger (no relation to Freddy) at Shriners Hospital in Springfield, Massachusetts, circa 1989, several years before the hospital dropped "for Crippled Children," from its name. Dr. Kruger died in 2003, but I still cling to my crutches every day.

After reading Anderson's article, my inner arms felt numb. Was this psychosomatic? Bodily symptoms caused by mental disturbances sounds about right. Just because crutches are considered unhealthy doesn't make me want to stop using them. They are part of my everyday life. However, like walking with a prosthesis outside, I have taken crutching indoors for granted.

***

Every morning I swing my leg-and-a-half over the edge of the bed and grab my crutches leaning against the wall and the headboard. The crutches are stacked rubber underarm pad atop underarm pad, cracked like the craggy mountainsides of the brown peaks on the game of Life. The frame or uprights are not laminate, pressboard or particle board, but wood. The inside straight edges curve naturally around the hand grip and are connected by the wooden axillary support. The foam hand grip pads covering wooden dowels have the leathery look of an old man's face. The wood under the foam is unblemished, fresh from the factory finish. The hardware, stainless steel screws, wing nuts, and two barely visible tiny finish nails below the underarm pad still hold nicely. The lower frame and adjustable peg, with antique rubber crutch tip, is marred, dented, and scratched. Standing on one foot, I slip the crutches under my arms and move them, pendulum-like, a few feet in front of me, catapult leg and stump past the sticks, and land one foot on the carpet. Repeat. Again. This time my left foot lands on ceramic tile and the crutching continues until I'm standing in front of the toilet. Stand and pee or sit and pee? Standing means I need two hands and have to put all my weight on my armpits. I sit down because it requires less coordination. I just woke up. A few more "steps," turn the water in the shower stall on. Wait. Wait. Feeling warm water, I put my foot on the white shower mat and cradle crutches between counter and wall. Let go of towel hook, heel-toe it a few feet, open shower door, and lean in, trusting the shower seat will hold my freefalling weight. While seated, get wet and shampoo hair. Stand up on one foot and wash back and butt. I don't really hop anymore, but that doesn't mean I don't move while standing on one foot. Cleansed, I exit by stretching my foot over the shower stall threshold and onto the mat. Rising slowly, I shift my weight over my good leg and in one motion straighten myself up. I shimmy slide on the mat, close the shower door and stand on one foot while drying off. Every day, I crutch back into the bedroom, fall back on the bed, lean crutches back to their place, don the prosthesis, and get dressed.

Today, I sit on the edge of the bed and get dressed. Then I pick up the pair of crutches, grab a canvas bag with my notebook, journal, and pens, and crutch out to the car in the garage. I get in the car. The crutches ride shotgun. The edge of the seat cradles my right knee, leaving my stump hanging.

I stop at a gas station at the corner of Airport and Government in Mobile. I have trouble maneuvering the crutches out of the car. When I do, I feel a woman of color staring at me. While the tank is being filled, my roving eyes force her to avert her gaze. She's dressed very nicely, it's

Sunday. A brown-skinned boy sitting in a passing yellow bus stares. When I stare at him, he does not notice. He is focused on the cuffed-up pant leg of my blue jeans, wondering perhaps, what happened to my leg.

When I pull into the restaurant parking lot, I regret my decision to go legless. I sit in the car contemplating whether I should go in or just head home, streak intact. I decide that the writing experience outweighs any awkward stares. I put my back on the door and head into the restaurant, backwards. Once inside, I spin around and move forward, letting the door close behind me.

"I'm here for the Writers' Drink and Scrawl." The dark-haired waiter with the tie-dyed T-shirt says nothing, but gives me a head bob to the left, which leads to the table on my right.

The Writer's Guild president gestures for me to sign in.

"Sit wherever you want," she says, looking down at me, "If you feel comfortable moving around."

I sit down at a table for four and try to figure out what to do with my crutches. I carefully lean them against the chair next to me and the table. Statues of weakness. The waitress, very young, cute, and Asian American, comes over and provides a list of beers on tap.

"420" I say, the Sweetwater beer named, the brewers say, for an interstate.

My streak of 7,665 days without leaving the house without my leg on is broken.

The waitress brings my 420. I drink and breathe in cool bronze barley-hopped refreshment. In honor of the record, I savor my liquid trophy, pondering baseball and Guinness.

Guinness is, of course, the king of record keeping. And yes, it's the same Guinness as the almighty thirst-quenching Irish elixir. In 1955 Sir Hugh Beaver, chairman of Guinness Brewery, decided to publish a book of records. Originally, *The Guinness*

Book of Records was kept behind bars for bartenders to use to settle arguments. Guinness was also the most awesome book for eight- to thirteen-year-old boys in the 1970s.

Once I'm settled in the chair, I write a few lines of observation—like a pitcher getting warmed up in the bullpen before he heads to the mound.

Music Too loud, Pen on the floor, Squeaking kitchen door
The old man and I have the same shoe. He's wearing two.
The silence of things is blissful now
And that makes me smile

Most of the writers sit at one large table and talk among themselves. A few officers with the guild come by and introduce themselves, but nobody ever sits down to talk with me. Am I being unsocial, or are they? It really doesn't matter. We all came here to write, not socialize. I heard that inner voice and began writing about Bert Shepard.

***

The TV sportscaster's voice breaks my concentration. He is singing the praises of Daniel Nava, baseball's newest media darling. The day before, I'd watched Nava's first-at-bat in Major League Baseball for the Boston Red Sox. A first pitch grand slam into the Red Sox bullpen. He's now one of four major leaguers to hit a first-at-bat grand slam. Nava, I'm certain, will be honored in the near future for his entry into the records books with a trophy, plaque, or new car.

"To our stumps," I say softly, raising my glass into the air to Shepard. I'm toasting the end of 7,665 days without leaving the house without my leg on. As I finish my beer, I wrestle with my unsteadiness on one foot and contemplate a wheelchair or other alternative transportation. I don't know if my leg-less presence gives the other writers something to write about, but I can say that I'm not the same me without a prosthesis on in public. To remember the day, I slide the empty Samuel Adams Silver Anniversary glass into my canvas bag, offer a few thanks and goodbyes to the group, and one-leg-it to the exit.

Out on an Idiom Limb Looking for a One Night Stand

W. "If you're going to tell people the truth, be funny or they'll kill you."

"You'll get some leg tonight for sure," David Lee Roth's voice echoed as I bellied up to the bar at Peg Leg Pete's in P-Town. It was 1984, three years ago.

"Hair of the dog," I told the man behind the stick. I was a barfly before I was old enough to hold my liquor.

I cased the joint and then caught sight of her. The woman brought me to my knees. I thought about standing up and sticking my neck out to talk to her.

"Cool your heels," I remembered telling my younger self. "Let the grass grow under your feet a minute."

I had cold feet, but the idea of asking her out had legs. I was realistic, had both feet on the ground. I decided not to drag my feet and finally dipped my toe in the water to get my feet wet and asked the woman out. I was not expecting to fall head over heels. Dating was new to me, but I was finding my feet. I'd planned on following in someone else's footsteps, but I wanted to fly by the seat of my pants. Footloose and fancy free. I wanted to get a toe hold, then a foot hold, but I definitely didn't want to get started on the wrong foot. Finally, I got my foot in the door, and quickly got my sea legs and put my best foot forward.

"You look like a million bucks," was my opening one-liner.

I kicked up my heels when she said, "Take a load off." Betty and I sat at a claw-foot table near a couple of three-legged bar stools.

"I'm beginning to fall for you," I told her straight-up.

237

"You might get lucky if you play your cards right."

We shot the shit for a while.

"I captained a pirate boat off the coast of Somalia. We were gunning for freighters in my Johnson-powered johnboat."

"I'm just a working girl," she said.

"I'm a jack of all trades, master of none," I bragged.

"Well, bless your heart," she sighed.

We drank Left Hand Ales and took turns pulling the one-armed bandit. We hit the jackpot with a pair of one-eyed jacks and cashed in our chips for cash on the barrelhead. We hit it off so well we talked for hours on end. We uncorked a bottle of Frog's Leap Cabernet, a full-bodied wine with great legs.

"How come you're not three sheets to the wind yet?" she asked.

"I've got a hollow leg," I said.

"My foot," was her knee-jerk reaction.

"I'm not pulling your leg." I jacked up my pant leg to show her.

"Cost me an arm and a leg, but without this prosthesis I don't have a leg to stand on."

Out of the blue, the bartender started muscling in on my action. He stepped on the wrong toes. Before I gave him the Ali one-two, I warned him to get off my back. I was dancing with two left feet, but I managed to float like a butterfly and sting like a bee. We went toe to toe until I got a leg up on the barman. He walked away with his tail between his legs.

"Don't ever set foot in here again," the bouncer said.

"Don't let the door hit you in the ass on the way out," the bartender yelled.

Betty gave me the go-ahead, so we took the show on the road, stretched our legs to the car, and I lead-footed it to her crib.

Back at her place, with the home field advantage, she was in her element. I was on my knees, with pins and needles, until she said, "Now you can sweep me off my feet." That's when she started getting a rise out of me. She had stars in her eyes and had given me the green light to take liberties. I used every trick in the book and took her for a ride.

"You're as cool as a cucumber," she cooed in my ear.

The next morning I woke up hung over, in a cathouse. Before I was back on my feet, I was looking for the exit, stage left. Suddenly, Betty was at my heels.

"I'm not a wham bam thank you ma'am, I'm the madam of the house," she cried.

I put my good foot down and told her to take a walk. "Goodbye," I said, and immediately realized I put my foot in my mouth. Betty was pissed off that I was leaving. We took up arms against one another. There was going to be a shootout.

I zeroed in on my target but I got hit first. I shot myself in the foot.

I was dead on my feet, on my last leg, with one foot in the grave.

"How's it feel when the shoe's on the other foot?" she said.

"I've made my own bed, dug my own grave," I said in cold blood.

She knocked me off by blowing me away with the kiss of death.

"You're the salt of the earth, Alan," Betty said, after I was deader than a doornail.

After I finally kicked the bucket, Betty buried me six feet under.

Street Writer

I spent Monday afternoon printing the chalk board sign "Fairhope" in yellow, "Street" in pink, and "Writer" in white on a green chalkboard. In the morning I packed a stainless-steel briefcase, which once contained a C-Leg microprocessor knee, with stuff I might need. I thought about not wearing a prosthesis that day. Most people stare, or sneak a peek at disabled people, but they avoid eye contact. There is a voyeuristic angle to this as people are curious about disability, but it also scares the heck out of some people. I didn't have the nerve to pull it off, but I wore shorts when I got in the car with my briefcase full of writing instruments, index cards, writing pads, my dictionary, thesaurus, and a broken clear-plastic container of rainbow-colored push pins.

I walked down the sidewalk to the bottom of Knoll Park and the misaligned intersection of Fairhope Avenue, South Mobile Street and Magnolia Ave. I had scouted the area the day before and decided the painted brown brick pedestals supporting a rugged overbuilt timber framed park shelter had good visibility, especially for people driving or walking up from the pier and the beach parking area. The covered area had raised brick pavers and a bench but I set up my chair with my left side toward traffic so my prosthesis would not be visible to every passing car. I unpacked a pen, my notebook, and clipboard.

I could not open the door to my room of thoughts. My heart was racing, my brown hair sweaty. I couldn't conjure up any inspiration. I was barely breathing because I was in a full-blown anxiety attack! All that for setting up a chair and taking out some pens. Ridiculous. I numbered the series on the top left, dated it top left, wrote out Fairhope Street Writer under my name and then scrawled FSW in the lower right-hand corner.

Limbs of live oak, needles of long pine,
Scents of honeysuckle and thyme.

I had to start somewhere. I couldn't connect with my surroundings. After I wrote each note, I grabbed a pushpin and walked to the front of the covered area, and pressed them into the wood for people to notice.

A woman walked past, headed down the hill toward the pier, and was getting ready to cross to street. She glanced back my way.

"Hey," I said, thinking this is my chance. Wait. I knew her. She used the computers at the library and once I sent a fax for her. She's petite, oval-faced like me, her hair was pulled back.

"What's this about?" she asked, walking closer.

"It's an experiment, kind of a writing exercise. I'm set up to write what I observe and to post it for others to see, read, and comment on. It probably sounds a bit crazy." I said it so fast it sounded like a salesman's pitch. She wheezed and squeaked simultaneously, like someone choking on a feather and stepping on a rubber duck at the same time. Apparently, I was funny.

"They say you should get out of your comfort zone," she said. I was so far out of my comfort zone, I was in outer space.

"Today was the day I was going to get stuff done," she said, but in a way that suggested she was happy to have walked past my writing booth. She sat down on the red pavers with the arch of her back resting on the brick column, chin on knee and hands clasped around her shins.

"I usually avoid people," she said, as I thought of my own introversions and shyness and wondered how I was even able to do this.

241

"I'm Leigh," she said, giving me her hand like a princess to a prince, "My last name is Allen," she said and I felt some deeper bond between us that most likely was not present.

"What do you think of the Fairhope Street Writer idea?" I asked.

"Well, it's interesting, but I think you picked the wrong spot." I picked the spot more for visibility than for people. I didn't tell her I was too scared to put my chair on a busy downtown corner on the first time.

"I originally planned to write something personal for people who came up to me," I told her, "but then I thought that might make strangers feel uncomfortable."

"Yeah, then I think people would think you were crazy," she said, and stood up to read the note cards I had push-pinned into the wood shelter.

"Take whatever one you like," I said, suddenly sensing a shortage of self-confidence.

"You mean I can take one and put it on my fridge at home?" How comforting, I thought. The fridge is such a prominent place. I would be honored to be on someone's fridge. That used to be where the great works of childhood went.

"I feel like I should give you something."

"I thought about putting out a tip jar, but for my first go-round I decided to let people take them."

Leigh took the first sentence I wrote.

A vivid spiritual wholeness illuminates the dark room
when a light shines from nothing.

For ninety minutes on a Tuesday afternoon, I was the Fairhope Street Writer.

***

Occasionally, you will find me continuing this creative endeavor closer to the library during outdoor art walks in Lower Alabama. Like a street poet in New Orleans, I'll write something about any subject. Look for my new title on the chalkboard sign.

"Stump the Librarian."

ALAN L. SAMRY

Epilogue-From Stumped to Superhero

X. "There's a three-legged coyote who lives up the hill from me. All the garbage cans in the neighborhood belong to him. It's his territory. Every now and then some four-legged intruder tries to take over. They can't do it. On his home turf, even a peg-legged critter is invincible."

Bywater, New Orleans, on a tour with the Slow Bicycle Society
on the Eastern Shore
Photo by Slow Biker and Librarian Valerie Stickney

245

A man in a Cinch T-shirt, missing his right arm, leans over the computer at the print station behind the reference desk. Cinch was spelled out in large serif letters below a man holding on to a bucking bronco. Around the cowboy on both sides were olive branches. The left sleeve of his Cinch T-shirt is empty, yet it looks full like a flag unfurled in a wind.

"What's Cinch?" I wanted to ask him, but didn't as he finger-curled me over to the station.

"The machine ate my twenty cents," he said.

"Sorry about that, but sometimes there's a glitch," I said, as I reached into the till to retrieve two dimes.
"The library's not trying to get rich one print job at a time," I added, hoping he could take a joke.

"No, that's what the copier's for," he said through a wide smile, "and that's where I'm heading next."

I didn't put this here because my next book is going to be about upper extremity amputees. I put it here to remind me how many people come into the library, or into our lives, or are already in our lives, who touch us in ways we don't think about. I can't write all the stories. You have to choose. I could write another book about Civil War amputees, celebrity amputees, athletic amputees, amputees with birth defects, or amputee veterans. I can't. I have to choose.

***

I met Beth from one of my coworkers at the library. A below-knee amputee, she was being bullied at school and her mom was really at a loss about how to help her. We talked at the library several times. She was a kind, energetic tween, who wore shorts and seemed comfortable with her leg, but at other times she seemed emotionally fragile. She was a huge fan of *Dolphin Tale*, and said she really enjoyed the book *Winter's Tail* too. Because I was a certified peer visitor with the Amputee Coalition, her mom insisted I come visit with Beth and the rest of the family at their home.

She had just had an amputation at Shriners Hospital in Georgia. Her mom, far enough away not to be lurking, but close enough to hear, just listened. Beth's brothers and sisters were bouncing off the sofa and loveseat, excited and curious about me.

We doffed our legs, each getting a close up look at our fates in life.

"I had five surgeries at Shriners," I told Beth, trying not to scare her, but she was curious about them, so I showed her the scars.

"These two were the biggies," I pointed to the end of my stump and the jagged scars that remain. "A bunch of years later, they took a pie shape of bone wedge out, right here, on the side below my knee, to straighten my stump."

Fighting back the tears, she said, "I have another operation. I'm scared," she said.

"Yeah, I know, I was scared too, but you know how much it hurts already," I say, trying to reassure her. "Having the operations when you are young means better fitting legs. You know why?"

"No," she whispered, as she wiped a tear from the side of her mouth.

"Because kids heal fast!"

"Yeah?"

"So fast, it's amazing!"

"Yeah, it took a few months," she remembered.

"If I had one of those surgeries now, it would take years for me to heal. These are things Mom's and doctors know best about."

"Plus, you want to know what the most important part is?"

"What?"

"Having your mom and dad and brothers and sisters around to help you through all this again." She looked around the room, and a minute later her dad pulled into the driveway.

I met her dad, and the afternoon quickly turned to evening. Beth's mom walked out to the front porch with me and thanked me for coming. She was worried as any mom would be about what the best decision was for her daughter. "Beth's gonna be okay," I told her, and as I glanced up at the long leaf pine in their front yard, I knew why. Nobody in my family treated me differently because of my 1.6 legs.

***

I'm creating a bookmark for our "online resources" and helping a man with a British accent find our new journals, *The Alabama Historical Quarterly* and *Alabama Review*, when up pops the Google Doodle for the day. It's the start of the Paralympic Games in Pyeongchang, Korea.

This year's competition is the biggest winter Paralympics to date, with more athletes and countries participating than ever before. More than 560 athletes will vie for more than 80 medals in six sports: alpine skiing, biathlon, cross-country skiing, Para ice hockey, snowboarding, and wheelchair curling. One US athlete, Brenna Huckaby, just appeared in the 2018 *Sports Illustrated Swimsuit Edition*. You should have heard some of the comments from the staff while I was searching out the latest issue. "It's for research," I said, "there's an amputee in it." Several coworkers took a look. Some said, "That's cool," and many were surprised it hadn't been done before.

A former coworker stops in with her daughter. Alice is famous around the library because, well, she's Laura's child. She had the best baby shower ever. Everyone on staff picked their favorite children's book, which became the core of baby Alice's library.

She's a curious one, always wondering about my leg ever since we ran up and down the hill under the live oak in our front yard. Keep in mind, I have pants on at the library, but there's no passing around her, she knows the real story.

"Alice always tells me she wants to go to Alan's library," Laura says. Alice calls me "peg leg," and it makes her mom uncomfortable, but I reassure her, that she's the only one I allow to do so. She's three. Still, she wants to know the answer that everyone wants to know. What happened to your leg? I try to tell her, but she's a very sharp little girl. After several attempts, I said, "One day you're going to learn about genetics and DNA and you'll understand all this." She tilted her head, puzzled. I tried a line I'd heard in a Josh Sundquist YouTube video that actually worked for him.

"Sometimes this happens to people." Alice is a future librarian, skeptic, and questioner of the world.

"Where's your leg? Your real leg?" Thank goodness, someone changed the subject.

Until Laura messaged me later, I didn't realize how magical my leg was. According to Laura, "Whether or not you believe it, Alice believes you are a superhero."

Alice spent an imaginary year as an elf-pirate from Peter Pan's world. Now she is "mostly a fairy," according to Laura. I had a pretty good imagination as a child, but Laura wrote to tell me that Alice "very much associates you with the magic she pretends to have."

It's like Alice visits Wayne Manor through the front door, and leaves through the library, which leads to, yep, you guessed it, the Bat Cave. To one little girl, I have my own public library, and I'm Stump: The Librarian!

"I can't find a copy of *The Gilded Age* by Mark Twain," a white-haired woman with freckles and next in line says.

"Let's take a look," I say. Walking past several fiction stacks, we turn left at the end of the aisle and skim for Twain.

"We've got two copies." I crack open the older book. "This one has the larger print."

"I'll take it."

In *S Is for Southern*, a fantastic reference book from the editors of *Garden and Gun* magazine, I was reading the Mark Twain entry. I had completely forgotten the wooden leg in *The Adventures of Huckleberry Finn*.

Speaking of classics, we have a local author, Becky Brunson, who is speaking about her book for a library program. Her parents bought and then tore down Harper Lee's childhood home in Monroeville, Alabama, and then they built the Hardee's Dairy Dream. Talking to Becky about her memoir, Lee, and the presentation she was going to share, I realized why I like learning and writing about amputees and why I will continue to do so. It's something I've tried to do all along, in life, in libraries, and in writing legs, but was now remembering from *To Kill a Mockingbird*. There is no better way to empathize with someone than to walk around in their shoe.

Bibliography

Y. "Give it up, Sub-Subs! For by how much the more pains ye take to please the world, by so much the more ye for ever go thankless!"

Abbott, John Stevens Cabot. *Peter Stuyvesant, The Last Dutch Governor of New Amsterdam*. New York. Dodd and Mead, 1873.

Albrecht, Gary L. *Encyclopedia of Disability*, Vol 1. Thousand Oaks, CA: Sage, Publications, 2006.

Adams, William Howard. *Gouverneur Morris: An Independent Life*. New Haven: Yale U. P., 2003.

Anderson, Hans Christian. *The Steadfast Tin Soldier*. New York: Alfred Knopf, 1986.

Baynton, Douglas. "A Silent Exile on this Earth." *The Disability Studies Reader*. 2nd Edition. Ed. Lennard J. Davis. New York: Routledge, 2006.

Baynton, Douglas C. "Disability and the Justification of Inequality in American History." *The New Disability History: American Perspectives*, edited by Paul K. Longmore and Laura Umansky, 33-57. New York: New York University Press, 2001.

Benchley, Peter. *Jaws*. New York: Ballantine Publishing, 1991.

Beston, Henry. *The Outermost House*. New York: Henry Holt and Co, 1988.

Brookhiser, Richard. *Gentleman Revolutionary: The Rake Who Wrote the Constitution*. New York: Free Press, 2003.

Burger, Jerry M. *Returning Home: Reconnecting with our Childhoods*. Lanham, Maryland: Rowman and Littlefield Publishers, Inc. 2011.

Burton, Virginia Lee. *Mike Mulligan and More: A Virginia Lee Burton Treasury*. Boston: Houghton Mifflin, 2002.

Cassel, Kay Ann and Uma Hiremath. *References and Information Services: An Introduction*. Chicago: Neal-Shuman. 2013.

Coogan, Thomas. "Disability in Literature." U of Leicester, England. 18 March. 2009, accessed 5/29/2011. Lecture.

Couser, G. Thomas. Disability, Life Narrative, and Representation." *The Disability Studies Reader*. 2nd Edition. Ed. Lennard J. Davis. New York: Routledge, 2006.

Couser, "Introduction" The Empire of the 'Normal': A Forum on Disability and Self-Representation." *American Quarterly*. 52.2 (2000) 305-310. JSTOR. Web. 30 April 2011.

Davis, Lennard J., ed. *Disability Studies Reader*. 2nd edition. New York: Routledge, 2006.

English, T. J. *Paddy Whacked: The Untold Story of the Irish-American Gangster*. New York: William Morrow, 2005

Fitzhugh, William W. and Elisabeth I. Ward, eds. *Vikings: The North Atlantic Saga*. Washington, DC: Smithsonian Institution Press, 2000.

Fletcher, Angus. "Introduction and Notes." *Treasure Island*. New York: Barnes and Noble Books, 2005.

Fries, Kenny, ed. *Staring Back: The Disability Experience from the Inside Out*. New York: Plume, 1997.

Garnet, Henry Highland. "Let Your Motto be Resistance," in *Let Nobody Turn Us Around: Voices of Resistance, Reform, and Renewal: an African American Anthology*.

Eds. Manning Marable and Leith Mullings. New York: Rowman and Littlefield Publishers, 2003.

Garnet, Henry Highland. *A Memorial Discourse*. Philadelphia: J.M. Wilson, 1865.

Garnet, Henry Highland. An address to the slaves of the United States of America. (rejected by the national convention, 1843) Lincoln, Nebraska: Libraries at University of Nebraska-Lincoln, 2007.

Garnet, Henry Highland. The Past and Present Condition, and the Destiny, of *the Colored Race: A Discourse delivered at the Fifteenth Anniversary of the Female Benevolent Society of Troy New York., February 14, 1848*. Miami, Florida: Mnemosyne Publishing Inc., 1969.

Gottheimer, Josh. Ripples of Hope: *Great American Civil Rights Speeches*. New York: Civitas Books, 2003.

Green, John. *The Fault in our Stars*. New York: Penguin Books, 2012.

Gutfleisch, Oliver, "Peg Legs and Bionic Limbs." *Interdisciplinary Science Reviews*, vol 28 no. 2 6/03 139-148,

Hall, Richard. *The World of the Vikings*. New York: Thames and Hudson, 2007.

Harman, Claire. *Myself and the Other Fellow: A Life of Robert Louis Stevenson*. New York: HarperCollins, 2005.

Haywood, John. *The Penguin Historical Atlas of the Vikings*. New York: Penguin Books, 1995.

Hine, Darlene Clark, William C. Hine and Stanley Harrold. *African Americans: A Concise History*. Upper Saddle River, New Jersey: Prentice-Hall, 2004.

Hochnadel, L. F. (2014, May). Miranda Cashin: Tall tales to sci-fi. *The O & P Edge*, pp. 70-71.

Horgan, Paul, *Conquistadors in North American History*. Greenwich, CT: Fawcett Publications, 1963.

Horwitz, Tony. *A Voyage Long and Strange*. New York: Henry Holt, 2008.

Hovde, Carl F. "Introduction and Notes." *Moby Dick*. New York: Barnes and Noble. 2003.

Hugo, Victor. *The Triggering Town: Lectures and Essays on Poetry and Writing*. New York: Norton, 1978.

Hutchinson, Earl Ofari. *Let Your Motto Be Resistance: The Life and Thought of Henry Highland Garnet*. Boston: Beacon Publishing, 1972.

Jameson, John F. *Narratives of New Netherlands, 1609-1664*. New York: Charles Scribner's Sons. 1909.

Jasinski, James. "Constituting Antebellum African American Identity: Resistance, Violence, and Masculinity in Henry Highland Garnet's (1843) Address to the Slaves." *Quarterly Journal of Speech* 93.1 (2007): 27-57.

Kaminski, John P., ed. *The Founders on the Founders: Word Portraits from the American Revolutionary Era*. Charlottesville, VA: University of Virginia Press, 2008

Kauffman, Bill. *Bye Bye Miss American Empire: Neighborhood Patriots, Backcountry Rebels, and Underdog Crusades to Redraw America's Political Map*. White River Junction, Vermont: Chelsea Green Publishing, 20110.

Kelly, James C., and Barbara Clark Smith. *Jamestown, Québec, Santa Fe: Three North American Beginnings*. Washington and New York: Smithsonian Books, 2007.

Kerouac. Jack. *On the Road*. New York: Penguin Books. 1997.

Kessler, Henry, and Eugene Rachlis. *Peter Stuyvesant and His New York*. New York: Random House, 1959.

King, Stephen. *On Writing*. London: Hodder and Stoughton, 2001.

Kirschke, James J. *Gouverneur Morris: Author, Statesman, and Man of the World*. New York: Thomas Dunne Books, 2005.

Klaus, Carl H. *The Made-up Self: Impersonation in the personal essay*. Iowa City: U of Iowa P, 2010.

Konstam, Angus. The History of Pirates. New York: Lyons Press, 1989.

Larson, Erik. *The Devil in the White City: Murder, Magic, and Madness at the Fair that Changed America*. New York: Crown Publishing, 2003.

Lee, Harper. *To Kill a Mockingbird: The 40th Anniversary Edition*. New York: Harper Collins, Publishers, 1999.

Lobel, Arnold. *On the Day Peter Stuyvesant Sailed into Town*. New York: Harper and Row: 1971.

Longmore, Paul K., and Lauri Umanski, eds. *The New Disability History: American Perspectives*. New York: New York University Press, 2001.

Mackay, Margaret. *The Violent Friend: The Story of Mrs. Robert Louis Stevenson*. Garden City, NY: Doubleday, 1968.

Magnusson, Magnus and Hermann Pálsson, Trans. *The Vinland Sagas: The Norse Discovery of America*. Penguin Books, 1965.

Marable, Manning and Leith Mulling, eds. *Let Nobody Turn Us Around: Voices of Resistance, Reform, and Renewal*. New York: Rowman and Littlefield Publishers, 2003.

Melville, Herman. *Moby Dick*. New York: Barnes and Noble Books, 2003. Print.

Miller, Melanie Randolph. *An Incautious Man: The Life of Gouverneur Morris*. Wilmington, Del: ISI Books, 2008.

Mitchell, David. "Body Solitaire: The Singular Subject of Disability Autobiography" The Empire of the Normal: A forum on Disability and Self Representation. *American Quarterly*. 52.2 (2000) 311-315. JSTOR. Web. 30 April 2011.

Mitchell, David. (1999) 'Too Much of a Cripple': Ahab, Dire Bodies, and the Language of Prosthesis in Moby Dick." Leviathan: *A Journal of Melville Studies*, 1:5-22. http://onlinelibrary.wiley.com. Web. 29 May 2011.

Mitchell, David and Sharon Snyder. "Narrative Prosthesis and the Materiality of Metaphor." *The Disability Studies Reader*. 2nd edition. Ed. Lennard J. Davis. New York: Routledge, 2006.

Moby Dick. Dir. John Huston. Perf. Gregory Peck, Richard Basehart. United Artists, 1956. DVD.

Moore, Dinty W. *The Truth of the Matter*. New York: Pearson Longman, 2007. Print.

Morris, Anne Cary, ed. *The Diary and Letters of Gouverneur Morris, Minister of the United States to France*. 2 vols. New York: C Scribner's Sons, 1888.

Moseley, Gabriel. "Ahab's Splintered Self." (2009) ECLS Student Scholarship. Paper 10. http://oxy.edu/ecls_student/10.

National Limb Loss Research and Statistics Program. Limb Loss in the United States. Amputee Coalition of America, 2007.

Nielson, Kim. "Historical Thinking and Disability History." *Disability Studies Quarterly* 28.3 (2008): 11pars. http://dsq-sds.org/. (Accessed Aug. 30, 2008).

Oates, Joyce Carol, and Robert Atwan, eds. *The Best American Essays of the Century*. Boston: Houghton Mifflin, 2000.

Ott, Katherine, David Serlin, and Stephen Mihm, eds. *Artificial Parts Practical Lives: Modern Histories of Prosthetics*. New York: New York University Press, 2002.

Otter, Samuel. (2006) "Introduction: Melville and Disability." *Leviathan: A Journal of Melville Studies*, 8: 7-16. http://onlinelibrary.wiley.com. Web. 29 May 2011.

Pasternak, Martin B. *Rise Now and Fly to Arms: The Life of Henry Highland Garnet*. New York: Garland Publishing, 1995.

Pearson, Judith. *The Wolves at the Door: The True Story of America's Greatest Female Spy*. Guilford, Connecticut: The Lyons Press, 2005.

Philbrick, Nathaniel. *Why Read Moby Dick*. New York: Viking, 2011.

Pliny the Elder: Natural History: A Selection. Trans. John F. Healy. New York: Penguin Books, 1991.

Pressfield, Steven. *The War of Art*. New York: Black Irish Entertainment, 2012.

Prose, Francine. *Reading Like a Writer: A Guide for People who Love Books and for those who Want to Write Them*. New York: HarperCollins, 2006.

Rapp, Emily. *Poster Child*. New York: Bloomsbury, 2006.

Richards, Penny L. "Online Museums, Exhibits, and Archives of American Disability History," *The Public Historian*, Vol. 27, No 2 (Spring 2005) 91-100.

Rogozinski, Jan. *Pirates, Brigands, Buccaneers, and Privateers in Fact, Fiction, and Legend*. New York: Facts on File, 1995.

Rollyson, Carl, and Lisa Paddock, eds. *Herman Melville A to Z: The Essential Reference to His Life and Work*. New York: Facts on File, 2001.

Roosevelt, Theodore. *Gouverneur Morris*. Boston: Houghton, Mifflin and Co., 1898.

Rosenbaum-Chou, T. (2013, Spring) "Update on osseointegration for prosthetic
  attachment." *The Academy Today: A Supplement of The O and P Edge*, pp.
  A9-A10.

The Sagas of Icelanders: A Selection. New York: Penguin Books, 2001.

Samry, Alan. "Three Legs of a Bedroom Life." *Disability Studies Quarterly*, 28:4 2008.

Samry, Alan. Shriners Hospital for Children. Springfield, Massachusettss, Patient Medical Records, Obtained: 2009.

Selznick, David. *The Invention of Hugo Cabret*. New York: Scholastic, 2007.

Shields, David. *Reality Hunger: A Manifesto*. New York: Alfred A. Knopf, 2010.

Shorto, Russell. *The Island at the Center of the World*. New York: Doubleday, 2004.

Simmons, Marc. *The Last Conquistador: Juan De Oñate and the Settling of the Far Southwest*. Norman, Oklahoma: University of Oklahoma Press, 1991.

Stevenson, Robert Louis. "My First Book—Treasure Island." *The Courier* 21.2 (1986): 77-88. http://surface.syr.edu/libassoc/206/.

Stevenson, Robert Louis. *Treasure Island*. New York: Barnes and Noble Books. 2005.

Sundquist, Josh. *Just Don't Fall: How I Grew Up, Conquered Illness, and Made it Down the Mountain*. New York: Viking. 2010.

Stuart, David O. *The Summer of 1787: the Men who Invented the Constitution*. New York: Simon and Schuster, 2007.

Stuckey, Sterling. "A Last Stern Struggle: Henry Highland Garnet and Liberation Theory." In *Black Leaders of the Nineteenth Century*, edited by Leon Litwack and August Meier, 129-147. Chicago: University of Illinois Press, 1991.

Taylor, Christopher. "The Limbs of Empire: Ahab, Santa Anna, and Moby Dick." *American Literature*. 83.1 (2011) 29-57. Online.

Thurston, A. J. "Pare and Prosthetics: The Early History of Artificial Limbs," Proceedings of the 2006 Cowlishaw Symposium ANZ Journal of Surgery Vol. 77 (December, 2007) 1114-1119. http://blackwell-synergy.com.

Toole, John Kennedy. *A Confederacy of Dunces*. New York: Wings Books, 1996.

Treasure Island. Dir. Byron Haskin. Perf. Bobby Driscoll, Robert Newton, Basil Sydney. Disney, 1950. DVD.

Tyson, Timothy B. *Blood Done Sign My Name*. New York: Three Rivers Press, 2004.

U.S Army Center of Military History. *Gouverneur Morris: Soldier-Statesmen of the Constitution: A Bicentennial Series*. CMH Pub. 71-22. 1986.

Vaswani, Neela. *You Have Given Me a Country*. Louisville, Kentucky: Sarabande. 2010.

Weise, Jillian. *The Amputee's Guide to Sex*. Brooklyn, NY: Soft Skull Press. 2007.

Whiting, Jim. *The Life and Times of Peter Stuyvesant*. Hockessin. Del: Mitchell Lane Publishers, 2008.

Winkelman, Diana Michele, "The Rhetoric of Henry Highland Garnet." M.A. diss. Waco, Texas: Baylor University. 2007.

Wood, James Playstead. *The Lantern Bearer: A life of Robert Louis Stevenson*. New York: Pantheon, 1965.

Woodward, Colin. *The Republic of Pirates: Being the True and Surprising Story of the Caribbean Pirates and the Man Who Brought Them Down*. New York: Harcourt Publishing, 2007.

Index of Amputees

Z. "The biological family isn't the only important unit in society; we have needs and longings that our families cannot meet."

This is only a partial list of amputees in the book. To see the full list, check out my Wiki page at stumpthelibrarian.com. Want to add your name to the list? Follow the instructions on the page.

261

Quote Sources

A. Aristophanes

B. Aimee Mullins

C. Hugo, *The Invention of Hugo Cabret*, by Brian Selznick

D. Author's adaption of a childhood memory aid

E. Henry Beston, *The Outermost House*

F. Italo Calvino

G. Bryan Stevenson, *Just Mercy*

H. Augustus Waters, *The Fault in our Stars*, by John Green

I. Pliny the Elder

J. Fitzhugh, William W., Elisabeth I. Ward, *Vikings: The North Atlantic Saga*

K. Tony Horwitz, *A Voyage Long and Strange*

L. Ralph Waldo Emerson

M. Montaigne, "Of a Monstrous Child"

N. Tom Joad, *The Grapes of Wrath*, by John Steinbeck

O. Isak Dinesen, *Out of Africa*

P. Stephen King, *On Writing*

Q. Butthole Surfers, "Pepper"

R.a, R.b, R.c, *On the Road*, Jack Kerouac

S. Neela Vaswani, *You Have Given me a Country*

T. Ignatius J. Reilly, *A Confederacy of Dunces*,
     John Kennedy Toole

U. Daryl Turner, KTVU News in Oakland, California, on his leg, emblazoned with the Oakland Raiders artwork, that was stolen from his front yard

V. Richard Hugo

W. Billy Wilder, screenwriter, movie director

X. Steven Pressfield, *The War of Art*

Y. From "Extracts," *Moby Dick*, by Herman Melville

Z. Gloria Steinem

ALAN L. SAMRY

Acknowledgements

My wife, Susan inspires me every day, and I'm so thankful for her love and support.

My siblings Lynne, Laurie, Mark, and Steve, friends, who have allowed me to share their lives and memories so I could tell my story.

John O'Melveny Woods and Judy Bishop-Woods at Intellect Publishing. Also, Ellie Lockett and Jasmine Hodges for their editing.

My readers along the way, including Leigh Allen, Donnie Barrett, Valerie Bouriche, Cheryl Bradley, Laura Counselman, Jack Daily, Tamara Dean, Megan Redlich, Rosalie Stromme, and Rivers Tilley.

Spalding University students: Martha Bourlakas, Angela Elson, Bill Goodman, and Sandi Hutcheson.

Teachers: Dianne Aprile, Bill Babner, Robert Callahan, Donald Devore, Donald Heines, Robert Finch, Patricia Foster, Frye Gaillard, Richard Goodman, Elliott Lauderdale, Molly Peacock, and Pauline Uchmanowicz.

My professors (Dr. John Burgess, Dr. Naomi Gold, Dr. Jamie Naidoo, and Dr. Steven Yates) and peers (Elevensies Cohort) in the School of Library and Information Studies (SLIS) online program at the University of Alabama.

Librarians not mentioned above, Rheena Elmore, and Falmouth Public Librarians Kathy Mortenson, Jill Erickson, and Adrienne Latimer. Valerie Stickney and Betty Suddeth are more than librarians, they are friends, as are all the people on this page and I'm sincerely thankful for their presence in my life.

CPSIA information can be obtained
at www.ICGtesting.com
Printed in the USA
BVHW031505130219
540211BV00002B/8/P